**总策划**

王晓辉 闵令超 王君校

**主　编**

许柏成

**纪录片主创**

刘鹏飞 冯　楠 台馨遥 付　朗 兰红超

马博瀚 司　诚 王安宁 孟　媛 周小骏

**特别感谢**

倪　军 安　地 南小林 丁志涛 付志斌

黄长奇 孙　雷

# 万象中国

# CHINA BOUQUET

## 第二册
## Book 2

许柏成 主编
杨 晗 编著

SinolinguA
华语教学出版社

First Edition 2024
Second Printing 2025

ISBN 978-7-5138-2513-9

Published by Sinolingua Co., Ltd
24 Baiwanzhuang Street, Beijing 100037, China
Tel: (86)10-68320585, 68997826
Fax: (86)10-68997826, 68326333
https://www.sinolingua.com.cn
E-mail: hyjx@sinolingua.com.cn
Printed by Beijing Hucais Culture Communication Co., Ltd

*Printed in the People's Republic of China*

# Preface

Culture, a key to enlightening one's mind, is crucial in promoting the exchanges between people worldwide. The short documentary series entitled *China Bouquet*, filmed by art.china.cn, an affiliate of china.org.cn, is a compilation of a multitude of short stories with a focus on Chinese culture. It presents the common but typical experiences of people from all walks of life to international readers.

*China Bouquet* is the epitome of Chinese culture, encompassing history, scenery, and culinary flavors and personages in their respective fields, such as the Liangzhu Cultural Ruins dating back over 5,000 years ago, quadrangle courtyard houses, China's tea drinks, purple clay pots favored by global tea drinkers, resurgent traditional makeup, mysterious women's scripts, the cooking method with a perfect blend of water and fire, delicious and healthy medicinal diet.

*China Bouquet* series is published in Chinese and English with appealing illustrations by Sinolingua after the documentary

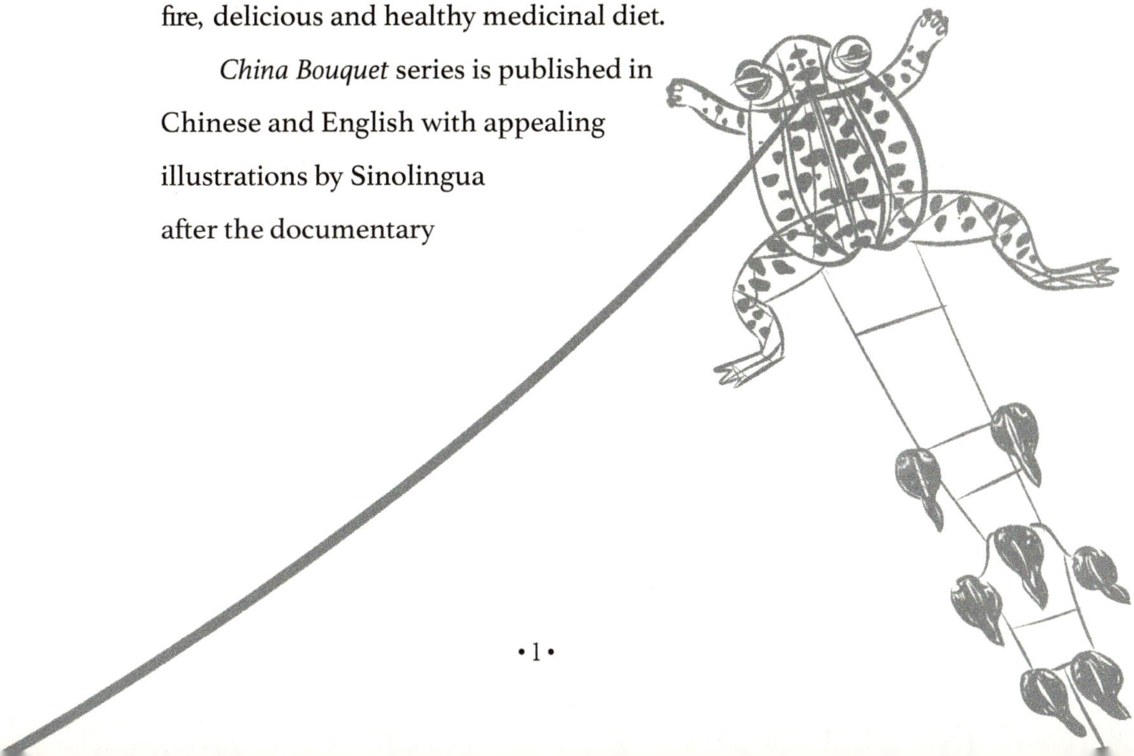

is offered online. The book series delves into Chinese values, cultural sense, and ethics behind each story. For example, "The Oldest Scent in China" depicts how Chinese people rely on natural forces to brew Yellow Rice Wine with dexterity. "Mega Rice Paper" shows how workers did their utmost to produce an 11-meter-long and 3.3-meter-wide "Mega Rice Paper". "New Scenes at Yungang" combines the early history of excavating the grottoes with the upgrading practices of a modern city, fully demonstrating how the Chinese maximize the use of resources to achieve sustainability. "Redefinition of Kung Fu" recounts how workers from different walks of life understand "kung fu"— the accumulation of time and sweat. Compared with the visually striking documentaries, the book series will bring you food for thought,

as if you were savoring green tea, leaving you with an endless aftertaste.

The series encompasses various stories, ranging from history to contemporary Chinese people's lives, through which the audiences can appreciate the unique aesthetics, philosophical thought, and ethics among Chinese to better understand Chinese people's code of conduct and life principles. Thanks to the effort of Sinolingua, the audiences can read the stories while watching the documentaries by scanning the QR code at the end of each story. This will enable international friends to know about China via one more type of media.

Xu Bocheng, Editor-in-Chief of art.china.cn from china.org.cn,<br>Chief Director of the Documentary China Bouquet<br>May 26, 2024

# 前言

文化如同一把开启心灵的钥匙，在世界各国人民交往过程中发挥着重要的作用。由中国网艺术中国拍摄的系列微纪录片“万象中国”聚焦中国文化，撷取具有代表性的元素，以小观大，通过一个个短小生动的故事向外国朋友介绍中国的各行各业，人生百态。

从5000年前的良渚遗址到今天仍烟火气十足的四合院，从中国人独特的饮茶品味到深受全球茶友喜爱的紫砂壶，从再度流行的传统妆容到一直神秘流传的女书，从巧妙调和了水与火的烹饪方式到既美味又有保健功效的药膳……“万象中国”系列纪录片从历史、风物、风味、人物等多个方面为观众呈现了一场中国文化的音画盛宴。

“万象中国”纪录片播出后，它的同名系列书由华语教学出版社以中英对照、图文并茂的形式出版。纸质图书重在发掘每一个故事背后中国人的价值观、文化内涵和精神品质。例如：《酒中深味》讲述中国人巧妙利用自然之力酿造黄酒的过程；《超级宣纸》讲述中国造纸工匠精益求精复原制作“三丈三超级宣纸”技艺的场景；《云冈新景观》将石窟开凿之初与今天城市更新的故事进行串联，体现中国人“物尽其用”的可持续发展思想；《功夫之道》则讲述了来自不同行业的劳动者对“功夫”的理解——时间与汗水的积累。相较于具有强烈视觉冲击效果的纪录片，纸质图书呈现出的是令人回味无穷的另一种传播效果，犹如一壶淡雅飘香的绿茶，清新、绵长。

“万象中国”将视角从历史深处回归当下中国人的日常生活，用讲故事的方式娓娓道来，观众和读者可以从中品味出中国人独特的审美情趣、哲学思想和道德观念，进而理解中国人的行为方式和处事原则。感谢华语教学出版社将传统出版与微纪录片巧妙融合，让读者在阅读的同时，还可以扫描每个故事结尾处的二维码收看该期微纪录片，让世界各国的朋友增加一个多媒介了解中国的窗口。

中国网艺术中国主编、纪录片“万象中国”总导演　许柏成

2024.5.26

# Contents
# 目　录

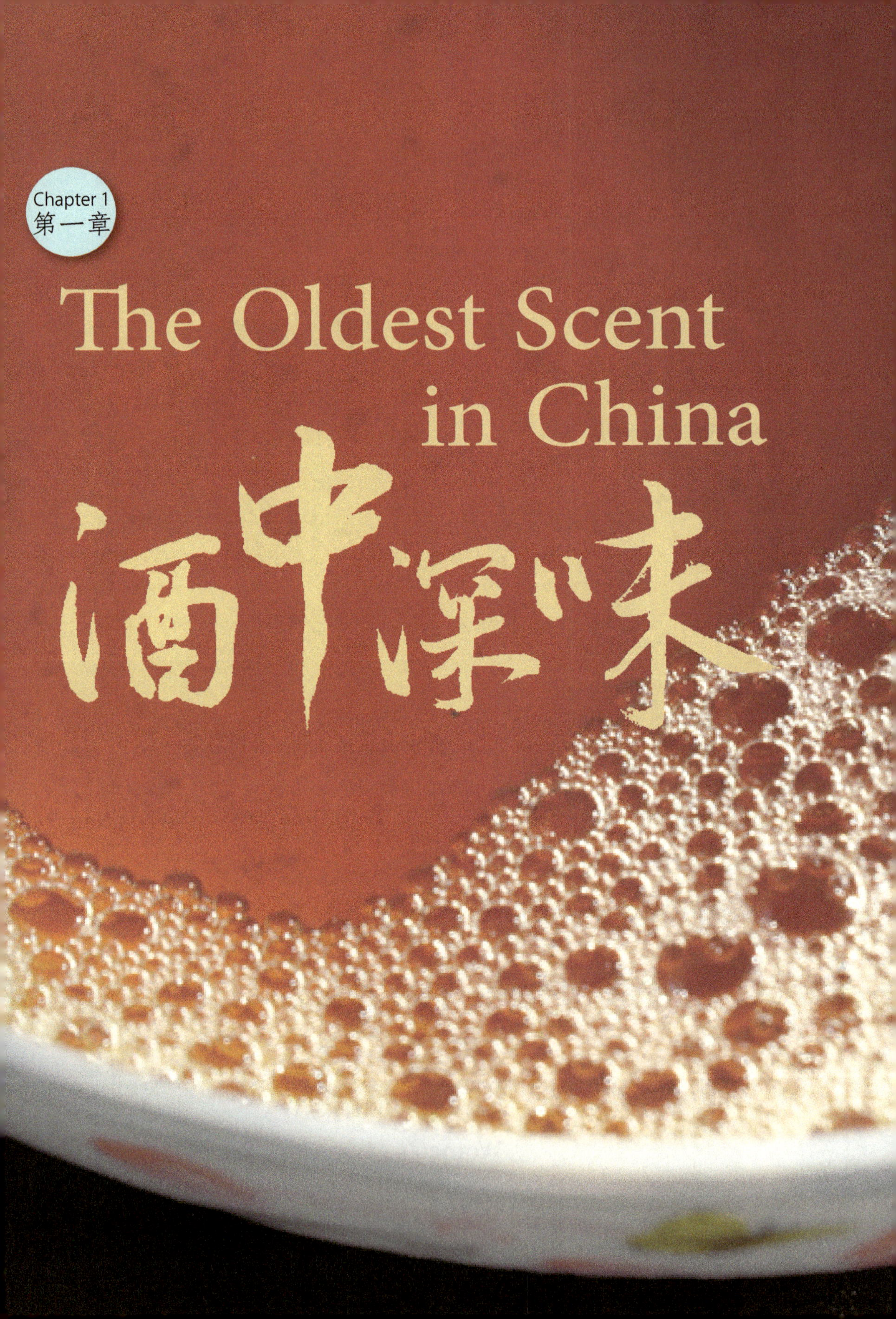

Chapter 1
第一章

# The Oldest Scent in China

# 酒中深味

万象中国
CHINA BOUQUET
第二册
Book 2

# The Oldest Scent in China

This is Hexin Village, surrounded by picturesque natural scenery, in Shaoxing, Zhejiang Province. Over two decades ago, Wang Mingzhong brewed several jars of Yellow Rice Wine for his newborn daughter. Today is the day he opens them. Wang moves an earthen jar weighing over 10 kg to the yard, where he removes its cover, bamboo band, and shell before retrieving a letter of good wishes. After he takes off the pottery cover, tears the oil paper, and removes the lotus leaves, the aroma of the wine emerges. Opening the wine jar is an indispensable ritual in Zhejiang when a daugher gets married. Wang becomes emotional when he holds the yellowed letter which has been sealed in the jar for over twenty years.

Upon the arrival of his daughter, Wang crafted wine as a symbol of his happiness and aspirations for her life ahead. As the seasons transitioned, the wine's initial sharpness faded, evolving into a velvety smoothness. Now, as his daughter steps into adulthood and prepares for marriage, he is about to partake in a tradition that has traversed at least 1,700 years: uncorking the wine made at a girl's birth during her wedding feast, affectionately known as "Daughter Wine".

At his daugher's wedding banquet, Wang enjoys the company of guests over shared drinks. Catching sight of the four characters 汪家兴旺 (wish the Wang family prosperity) inscribed on a yellowed letter, Wang breaks into a smile. In that moment, a dream harbored in the wine jar for over two decades is realized.

Shaoxing Yellow Rice Wine stands as a time-honored beverage with a rich heritage, encompassing a variety of types such as *yuanhong, jiafan, huadiao, shanniang* and *xiangxue* wines, all of which are widely recognized by the public.

Among these, *yuanhong* wine is a particularly popular variant. It derives its name *yuanhong* (literally red) from the red earthenware jar used by the host family to store the brewed Yellow Rice Wine. Characterized by its complete fermentation, this wine boasts a lower residual sugar content, resulting in a clear, bright appearance and a distinctive aroma. It offers a mild yet slightly bitter taste. Thanks to its ability to be stored for extended periods, *yuanhong* wine enjoys a broad appeal.

In Shaoxing, a traditional practice among families involves burying a jar of wine underground to commemorate the birth of a child. When the child is a boy, the parents nurture hopes of him working diligently, aspiring for him to share the buried wine with the villagers upon attaining professional success. This wine is named *Zhuangyuan Hong*, which translates to Champion's Red, symbolizing high achievement. On the other hand, if the newborn is a girl, the wine is called *Nu'er Hong*, or Daughter Wine, reserved to celebrate her wedding day with friends and family.

Yellow Rice Wine, distinctive to China, is esteemed as one of the world's renowned ancient liquors, alongside beer and wine. Shaoxing boasts ideal conditions for brewing Yellow Rice Wine due to the optimal natural materials of water and rice found here.

Nature is like a magician, giving us Jianhu Lake, a sanctuary pivotal for sustaining food abundance. Just as the saying goes, "water is the lifeblood of wine," the essence of crafting exquisite wine lies in the purity of its water. Sourced from Kuaiji Mountain, this water undergoes a natural purification process through layers of rock and sand, rendering it perfect for brewing Shaoxing Yellow Rice Wine. The unique characteristics of Jianhu Lake's water are indispensable for producing the distinguished Shaoxing Wine, elevating it to its high quality. Moreover, Jianhu Lake's influence extends beyond wine, enriching Shaoxing with an abundance of food. When it comes to wine-making, the calibre of the ingredients triumphs over the methodology. Without superior ingredients, no fine wine can come into existence. Therefore, glutinous rice stands as a crucial component for crafting premium Yellow Rice Wine. Historically, Shaoxing's glutinous rice has been indispensable for producing this yellow wine due to its high starch content, strong stickiness, ease of steaming, rapid fermentation, and efficiency in production, earning it the nickname the "meat of the wine".

The beginning of winter marks the start of the days when Shaoxing people brew the Shaoxing Yellow Rice Wine. Over the past hundreds of years, the period starting from the beginning of winter to the beginning of spring the next year has been considered the optimal time for brewing Yellow Rice Wine by Shaoxing people. Weather changes at different time while soil conditions vary as the climate changes. Because of the low temperature, clear water and stable water quality in winter, the growth of bacteria can be effectively curbed, ensuring smooth wine fermentation. Additionally, the fermentation at a low temperature for a long period in winter helps form a good flavor. Therefore, winter is the best time to ferment the wine, which is why Shaoxing Yellow Rice Wine is brewed during this time.

In the past, on the day marking the beginning of winter, the wine workshop in Shaoxing would hold a ritual to make a sacrifice for the God of Wine. The ritual scale is related to the size of the workshop. A common wine maker or a small workshop would only offer sacrificial items in front of the God of Wine, such as livestock, pastries and joss sticks and candles. Over time, this activity evolved into a local wine-making festival in Shaoxing.

Besides high-quality water and rice, the sophisticated brewing technique is indispensable. The techniques of brewing Yellow Rice Wine have become increasingly complicated through generations, including screening and soaking rice, steaming, cooling, preparing, fermenting, stirring, fermenting after sealing the jar, squeezing and heating. Scientific principles are needed to be engaged in each process. Take fermentation for example; the wine-maker needs to have a good command of the fermentation process and make timely adjustments according to the temperature, quality of rice, yeast, and wheat koji. In fact, without over a decade's experience, it would be impossible to master the single fermentation technique. The essence of Yellow Rice Wine lies in the inheritance of the craftsmanship of winemakers from generation to generation.

Taking advantage of the low temperature of the early winter morning at four o'clock, Guo Qirui stirs the steamed rice that was made the night before. Stirring is the process of exhausting carbon dioxide from the fermented rice and delivering fresh oxygen. Temperature is important. High or low temperature will affect the quality of rice saccharification and fermentation. With the rhythmical stirring, the rice under the influence of the yeast, wheat koji, water and air begins its journey towards becoming wine. According to the ancient brewing methods, there are over 30 different steps to brew a jar of Yellow Rice Wine. Though the process is complex, these winemakers still operate with hands believing that the touch and feel of human hands is exactly what makes wine great.

What remains is the passage of time. The wine will lie undisturbed in the darkness inside the pottery jar. Jars allow the wine to breathe. They will be left here to pass through the winter. Once the wine is brewed and sealed, it continues to ferment, awaiting the right moment.

Guo Qirui, a senior winemaker, devotes his lifetime to the career. He says, "I think the wine is alive. At 8 or 9 o'clock in the evening, when everyone's work is done and they have all gone, I take a look around and listen to the sound in the jar. The sound warms my heart."

The Yellow Rice Wine has a mellow, sweet and sour taste, but it is not overpowering. In southern China, the wine is often used to cook gourmet foods, such as *huadiao* chicken, drunk shrimp, and drunk crab. *Huadiao* chicken is one of the typical dishes in which Yellow Rice Wine is added. When cooking the dish, you will find the kitchen full of a pleasant aroma. The combination of wine mellowness and the tenderness of chicken will produce a marvelous flavor. This dish is a must-have to treat guests by Shaoxing people.

Southern China's winter is cold and humid. The Yellow Rice Wine is traditionally warmed to entertain the guests to drive away the winter chills and to warm the soul.

# 酒中深味

浙江省绍兴市合心村是一个山清水秀的小山村。二十几年前，汪明中为自己刚出生的女儿酿制了数坛黄酒，今天是将它们开坛的日子。汪明中开心地把重达二三十斤的土坛子搬到院子里，开坛口，解藤条，开箬壳，取出一封祝福信，取下灯盏，撕开油纸，打开荷叶——一股酒香扑面而来。女儿红开坛，这是浙江百姓嫁女儿时不可忽视的仪式。老汪捧着二十几年前封在坛口、现在已经发黄的信，感慨万分。

当年，汪明中在女儿出生之际亲手为女儿酿酒以表达心中的喜悦和对未来生活的祈愿。而今，四季轮转二十载，坛里的酒已经脱去稚气，女儿也已经长大成人，即将出嫁。这种女儿出生时酿酒、出嫁时开坛庆祝的习俗在当地已经流传了至少1700年，这种酒有个美好的名字——女儿红。

在女儿的婚宴上，老汪与宾客把酒言欢。看着发黄的信纸上的“汪家兴旺”这四个字，老汪满脸笑容——二十多年前随黄酒封进酒坛里的愿望实现了。

绍兴黄酒是流淌千年的醇香传奇。它的种类繁多，元红酒、加饭酒、花雕酒、善酿酒、香雪酒等，都是人们比较熟悉的品种。

元红酒是绍兴黄酒中最基本的一种酒。古时，宴客者将自家酿造的上好黄酒装在涂成朱红色的坛里招待宾朋，“元红”因此而得名。元红酒存放时间长，发酵较完全，含糖量较少，又经过多年的沉淀，酒色橙黄且透亮清澈，散发出独特的芳香，口感甘爽，略带苦味，因此受到人们的喜爱。后来，绍兴的百姓家在婴儿诞生之时都会准备一坛黄酒藏于地下：如果是男孩儿，希望他勤于读书，待取得功名返乡之时，便将老酒从地底挖出以招待亲朋好友，这种黄酒称为“状元红”；如果是女孩儿，这坛精心准备的黄酒便称为“女儿红”，待女儿出嫁之时宴请亲友。

与啤酒、葡萄酒并称世界三大古酒的黄酒为中国所独有。中国浙江省的绍兴市拥有酿造黄酒得天独厚的条件，那里的水源和稻米可以提供优质的天然原料。

大自然像一位魔术师，它创造出了鉴湖，创造出了绍兴的鱼香谷丰。俗话说：“水为酒之血。”没有好水怎能酿出好酒？由于鉴湖水源出于会稽山区，湖水经岩层、沙砾等过滤净化，水体清洁无污染，且硬度适中，为酿造绍兴黄酒提供了良好的先决条件。“汲取门前鉴湖水，酿得绍酒万里香。”离开了鉴湖水，也就很难酿出优质的绍兴酒了。可以说，鉴湖水很大程度上成就了绍兴酒。也因为有了鉴湖，绍兴成了鱼米之乡。好酒是酿出来的，更是种出来的。酿好酒，必须有好原料；酿好黄酒，必须有好糯米。在历史上，上等绍兴黄酒必以优质绍兴糯米酿造。这是因为绍兴糯米具有淀粉含量高、黏性强、蒸煮易、发酵快、出酒率高等优点，被形象地比喻为“酒之肉”。

每年立冬，是绍兴人开始酿造黄酒的日子。千百年来，绍兴人把从立冬开始到第二年立春这段最适合酿制黄酒的时期称为“冬酿”。“天有时，地有气”，冬季气温低，水体清冽，水质

稳定，可有效抑制杂菌繁育，确保酿酒发酵顺利进行，又能使酒在长时间发酵过程中保持低温，从而形成良好的风味，是酿酒发酵最适合的季节，所以绍兴黄酒主要在这段时间酿制而成。

过去，每逢立冬这一天，绍兴民间酿酒作坊都要举行祭祀“酒神”的仪式。仪式规模与作坊大小有关，一般酿酒小户和小作坊只是在“酒神”像前供奉一些祭品，如家畜、糕点、香烛等。后来，这种民间活动逐步演变成演绎绍兴酒俗和风情的“开酿节”。

除了好水和好米，酿出好酒还需成熟的酿酒工艺。绍兴黄酒的酿造技艺经历代发展变得日益复杂，有筛米、浸米、蒸饭、摊冷、落作、主发酵、开耙、灌罐后酵、压榨、煎酒等工序，而每一道工序都是一门科学。以发酵工序为例，酿酒师傅要根据气温、米质、酒酿和麦曲性能等多种因素灵活掌握发酵过程，及时调整。仅这一道工序，酿酒师傅没有几十年的经验是掌握不了的。酿酒师傅的经验和手艺世代相传正是绍兴黄酒的精髓所在。

凌晨4点，趁着深冬清晨的低温，酿酒师傅郭启瑞为前一晚落作的蒸饭进行第一次开耙。开耙是为发酵中的米水排出二氧化碳并输送新鲜氧气的过程。温度的掌握至关重要，或高或低都会影响糯米糖化发酵的品质。在酿酒师傅有规律地上下搅动中，糯米在酒母、麦曲、水和空气的作用下开始了变化之旅。一坛黄酒的诞生要历经30余道工序——那是一套传承有序的古法。尽管工序烦琐，但酿酒师傅坚持采用手工操作。他们洗净双手，亲自耙米，因为他们相信人手的感觉和经验可以为酒注入生气。

全部工序完成后，接下来，交给时间。在陶坛包裹的一小方黑暗里，酿好的酒将在此静静地经历一整个冬季。陶坛使酒能够呼吸。封坛后，酒仍在悄悄改变，越陈越香，等待着那个被唤醒的时刻。

郭启瑞是黄酒高级酿造师，他对酿酒倾注了毕生的心血。他说："我就觉得这酒是有生命的。晚上八九点钟，车间里的人结束了一天的工作以后都走了，我会自己再去转一圈，听听缸里面

的声音，很有感觉，很不错的。”

黄酒性情平和，口感酸甜舒爽，不喧宾夺主。在中国江南的饭桌上，人们也常巧用黄酒烹饪美食，制作花雕鸡、醉虾、醉蟹等各色菜肴。其中，花雕鸡是黄酒入菜的代表。在制作的时候，整个厨房充盈着馥郁迷人的清香，花雕酒的醇厚与鸡肉的鲜香相结合，会产生奇妙的香味。这道菜是绍兴人待客的必备佳肴。

江南的冬季潮湿阴冷，温一壶黄酒招待乡亲或与家人共聚时啜饮，可以为身体去除一整个冬季的寒湿，让味道和心意流转。

SCAN FOR A VIDEO

Chapter 2
第二章

# Magic Chopsticks

# 神奇的筷子

万象中国
CHINA BOUQUET
第二册
Book 2

# Magic Chopsticks

What is the symbol of Chinese food? Chopsticks could be counted as one!

There are many legends about the origin of chopsticks. One reliable legend goes as follows: While passing by three times, Yu the Great avoided entering his home for the sake of controlling the flood. Therefore, he had to eat food in the wilderness. As the beast meat that was just cooked was too hot to grasp with hands, Yu incidentally broke a tree branch and ate the meat and rice with it. This is believed to be the earliest form of chopsticks.

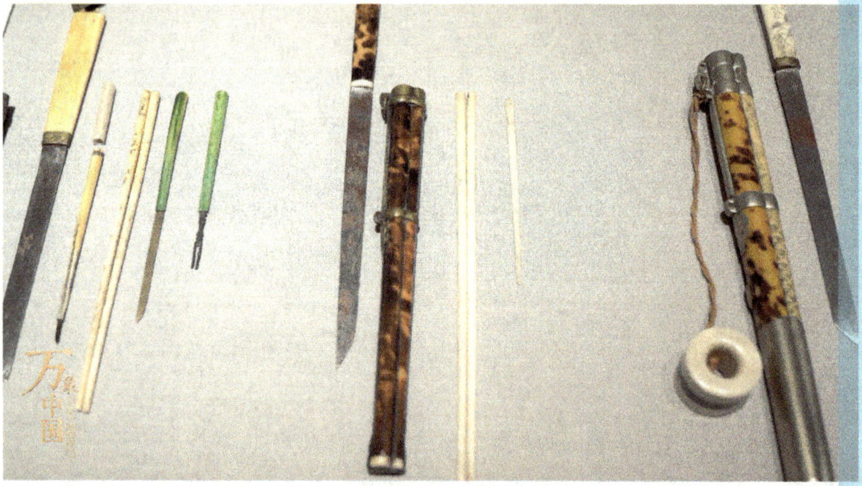

Originally, chopsticks were called 箸 (zhǔ). During the sacrificial rituals of the pre-Qin period, a pair of bamboo chopsticks would be inserted into the cooked food for the ancestors to enjoy. 煮 (zhǔ), which means cooked, is the same as the ancient character 者 (zhě). Since the chopsticks are often made of bamboo, the radical ⺮ (meaning bamboo)

was put on top of the character 者. And thus, the character 箸 came into being.

Why did 箸 evolve into 筷 (kuài) later? This is related to the folk taboo prevalent in the region south of the Yangtze River during the Ming Dynasty (1368-1644), where boats frequently weaved across myriad rivers and lakes. 箸 is a taboo word the boatmen and fishermen in

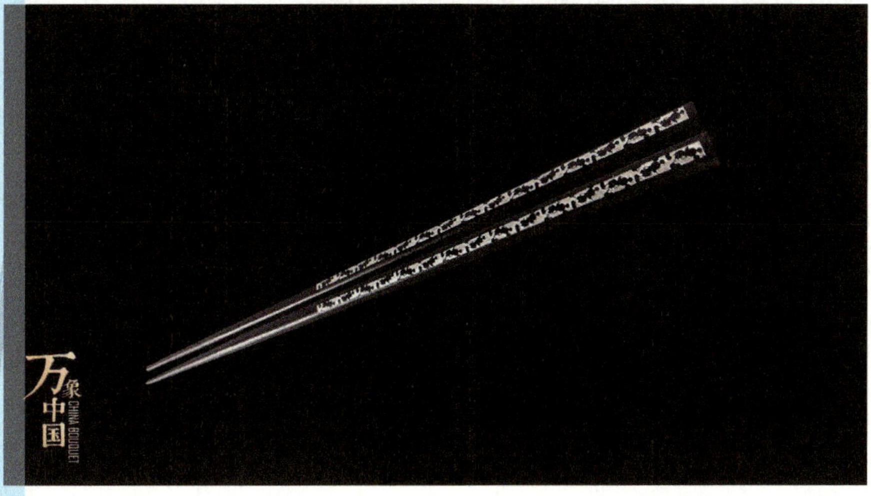

Wuzhong District especially avoided because 箸 is a homophone of 住 and 蛀, which means "stop" and "moth-eaten", respectively. What they feared most was that there would be no business in case of the stoppage of boats. Even worse, if their boats were eaten by moths and thus leaked water, how would they catch fish in their boats? Therefore 箸 was changed into 筷, a homophone of 快 meaning "fast", with the hope that boats move fast with good fortune. Afterwards, 筷子 spread far and wide.

Hotpot, *dandan* noodles, dumplings, stinky tofu, Kung Pao chicken .... The art of handling the magically dexterous chopsticks should not be neglected to enjoy such a huge variety of regional cuisines and culinary styles.

If you want to use chopsticks well, start by training flexibility in your fingers and wrists. This differs from knives and forks, which require more force in the arms. China's agricultural history has given its people dexterous hands. Farming, mulberry picking, weaving, and embroidery made those fingers extra sensitive. With these fingers and wrists moving in tandem with two sticks, people can easily complete many actions such as stirring, mixing, picking, pricking, cutting, clipping, plucking, and scraping.

Li Dongsheng is a designer of chopsticks and founded a museum of chopsticks in Linhai, a thousand-year-old city in Zhejiang Province. Some people collect antiques, and others collect paintings, but he has found a passion for chopsticks and has been designing and collecting chopsticks for 16 years.

Li Dongsheng said, "My collection dates back to the Han Dynasty (206 BC-AD 220). From the Han Dynasty to the Tang Dynasty (618-907), each one was served with separate utensils at banquets. They sat on the floor with plenty of space, feasting on the food while enjoying the song and dance. The chopsticks which were cast in bronze in that

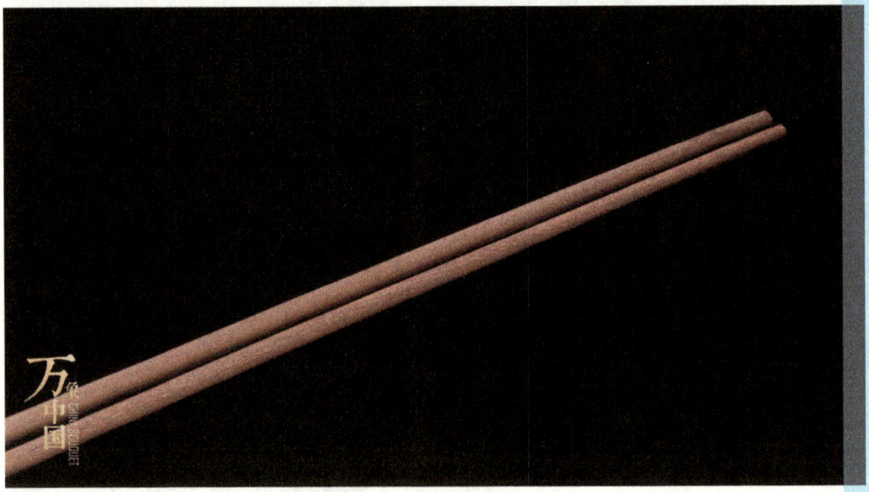


period have been well preserved. In the Han Dynasty, chopsticks were also made with lacquer, wood, and bamboo. Since these materials are easily decayed, these chopsticks cannot be kept till now. The chopsticks used in the Tang Dynasty and before were longer and thinner compared with those of today. In the Song Dynasty (960-1279), chopsticks became simpler. The upper end of chopsticks became square, and the lower end for picking up food was rounder. The modern Chinese chopsticks were basically formed from that time."

For ordinary Chinese, a pair of bamboo or wooden chopsticks is better suited for their daily needs. Their flexibility enables craftsmen to use their skills to draw exquisite designs on its small shaft by chiseling, cutting, or carving out detailed patterns. Li enjoyed local popularity due to his excellent carving skills.

From a strip of bamboo to this simple shape, the creation of a pair of chopsticks goes through numerous steps. One end being square and the other round symbolizes the old idea that the Earth was square and Heaven was round. China's natural red lacquer is known as the "king of paint". When applied to high-quality wood, a pair of chopsticks is said to last thousands of years.

Over the course of their development, the chopsticks have gradually taken on more cultural connotations. For example, the standard length of chopsticks is 7 *cun* 6 *fen* (about 25 cm), which symbolizes seven emotions and six sensory pleasures that distinguish

humans from animals. A standard chopstick features one end that is square and the other that is round, symbolizing the round Heaven and square Earth. Just as the Heaven is considered the most important, people regard food as their primary need. This is why chopsticks have such a form. Additionally, chopsticks always come in pairs, though the term "two chopsticks" is never used. This is attributed to the unique notions of Tai Chi and yin yang held by Chinese people, which propose that one and two can mutually convert and integrate. Chopsticks, a daily necessity for the Chinese, are imbued with traditional Chinese philosophy and wisdom.

Chopsticks serve as the bridge connecting people with food, as well as facilitating interpersonal connections. They can be used not only as eating utensils, but also as gifts. In the past, chopsticks were part of a daughter's dowry because in Chinese, "chopsticks" (筷子) have a pronunciation similar to 快子, which means "quickly giving birth to a child after marriage." Friends would make a promise by breaking chopsticks, pledging their allegiance to achieving success through concerted effort. Additionally, ten pairs of chopsticks convey the cultural sense of perfection and reunion. Chopsticks given to business partners indicate long-lasting cooperation, as wood makes the woods. Chopsticks have long been an indispensable part of Chinese people's daily life.

The chopsticks are the primary eating utensils used by the Chinese, who must adhere to certain rules when using them. Before sitting at the dining table, children receive their first lesson on how to use the chopsticks under the guidance of their parents. During a banquet or meal, the way one uses chopsticks epitomizes their etiquette, reflecting a person's culture and manners. There are many taboos associated with using chopsticks. For instance, it is considered improper to drop them on the floor during a meal, to make noise with them while eating, or pass a bowl of rice with chopsticks inserted into it to someone else. Indeed, a pair of chopsticks showcases the cultural depth of China as a nation of ceremonies.

Since ancient times, chopsticks have been symbols of luck and peace. A pair of chopsticks is straight and neat, with round and square ends. Confucius once said, "The value of rituals lies in making people live in harmony." Around the dining table, Chinese people only pick up food in front of themselves rather than that of others, which exemplifies the notion proposed by Confucius.

# 神奇的筷子

若问中餐的标志是什么？筷子，或许可以算作一个。

关于筷子的来源，传说有很多，下边这个比较可信：相传大禹在治理水患时曾三过家门而不入，他平时只能在野外进餐，刚烧煮熟的兽肉太烫无法用手抓起来吃，于是大禹急中生智，随手折了树枝用来夹肉和米饭。这就是最早的筷子的雏形。

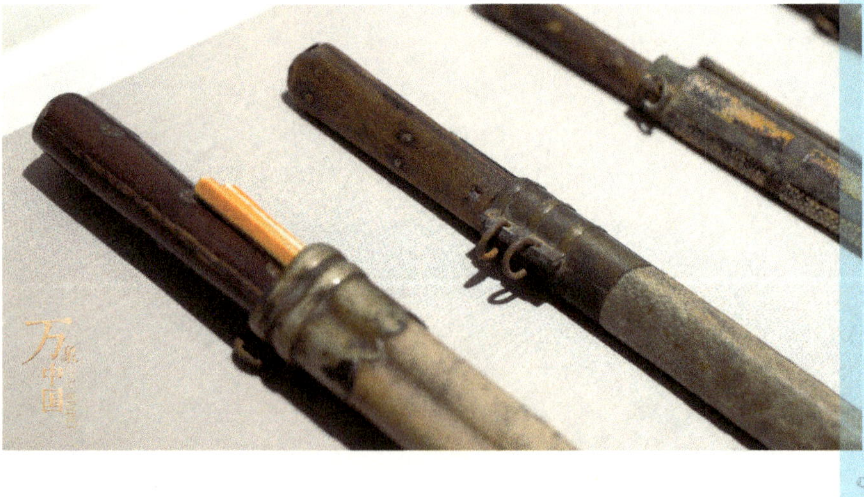

筷子最开始叫作“箸”。先秦祭祀时，常在煮熟的食物上插一双竹筷，以便祖先享用。“煮”和“者”在古代是同一个字，因为筷子是用竹子制成的，于是人们形象地创造了一个字——箸。

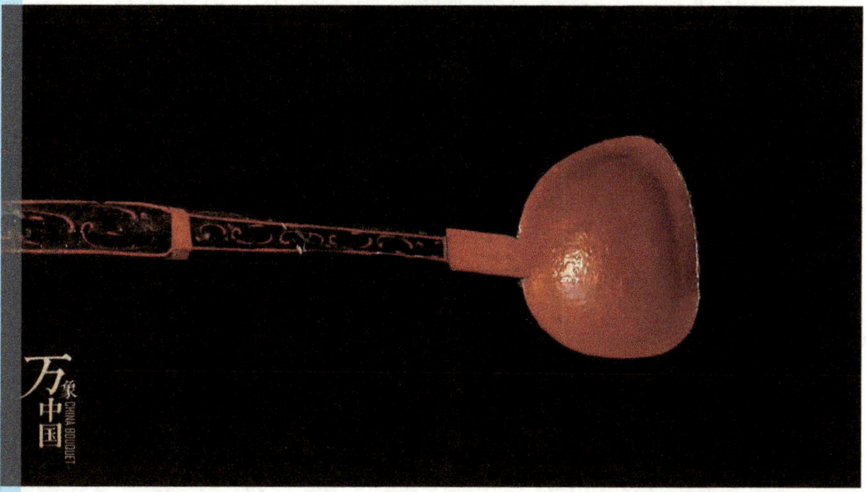

“箸”演变为“筷”，与明朝时江南水乡的民俗讳言有关。江南多河道，船只往来频繁，吴中船民和渔民特别忌讳“箸”，

因为“箸”字与“住”同音，他们最怕船“住”，船停住了，就没有生意可做；他们更怕船被虫“蛀”，木船被蛀了会漏水，如何行船、捕鱼？所以，他们便将“箸”改为“筷”，以求“快”行，图个吉利。久而久之，“筷子”之名便流传开来。

火锅、担担面、饺子、臭豆腐、宫保鸡丁……中国地域广阔、菜系派别多样，人们能品尝如此多的美食，筷子功不可没。

如果你想用得一手好筷子，要从训练手指与手腕的灵活性开始。这和刀叉更多运用手臂的施力方法不同。农耕文明给了中国人一双灵巧的手。耕种、采桑、纺织、刺绣，手指在漫长而精细化的自然劳作中变得日益灵敏。依靠手指、手腕与两根木棍的合作，每个人都可以轻松完成搅、拌、挑、扎、截、夹、拨、刮等诸多就餐动作。

李东升是一名筷子设计师，他在浙江省临海市建造了一座筷子博物馆。有人收藏古董，有人收藏字画，做了16年的筷子设计的他，则一路收藏这日常离不了的、再平常不过的筷子。

李东升说：“我收藏的筷子中最久远的是汉代的，从汉代到唐代期间，中国的宴席采用的都是分食制，人们席地而坐，一人一案一套餐具，边欣赏歌舞边享用美食。那时使用的筷子只有青铜材质的才得以遗存下来，当然汉代也有漆筷、木筷和竹筷，但这些材质都易腐，很难保存到现在。在形制上面，唐代及以前的筷子都偏长、偏细，到了宋代就变得比较简约，上面方，入口那一部分偏圆，中华筷的制式从那个时候开始慢慢形成了。”

对普通的中国百姓来说，一双竹筷或木筷更能满足日常所需。竹和木具有良好的可塑性，以此为业的匠人更能在筷子小小的体积上制作出精美的纹饰，或凿、或削、或雕、或刻。李师傅凭借一手雕刻筷子的功夫在当地小有声誉。

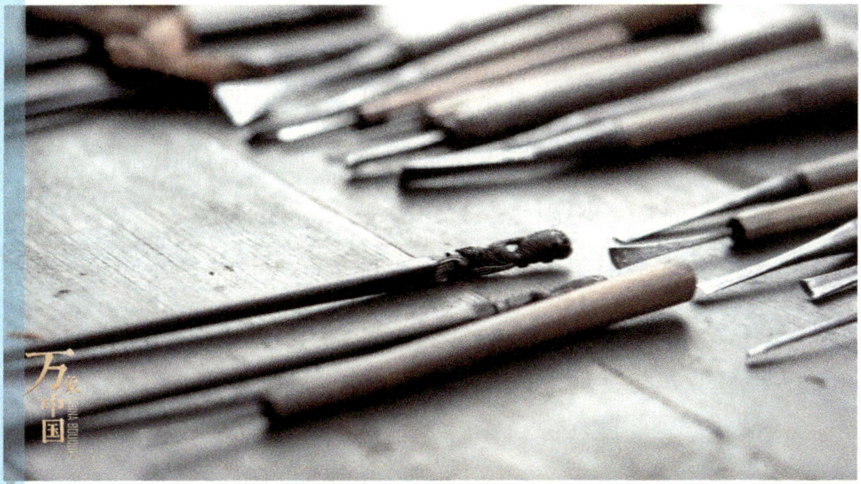


一双筷子的诞生经历了无数次删繁就简。上方下圆，象征天圆地方。长短粗细，需要反复打磨。中国的天然大漆素有“涂料之王”的美誉，把它涂在取材考究的木料上，一双筷子便可以千年不腐。

在漫长的发展过程中，筷子被中国人赋予了太多的文化象征。比如，筷子的标准长度是七寸六分，代表着人是有七情六欲的，以示人与动物是有本质区别的。又比如，标准的筷子一头方一头圆，象征着天圆地方。乾为天，为第一，民以食为天，由此而来。再比如，筷子明明是两根，但我们从来不会说“两根筷子”，而是说“一双筷子”，这种说法体现了中国人独有的太极和阴阳的理念。太极是一，阴阳是二；一就是二，二就是一；一中有二，合二为一。这是中国人的哲学。中国人每天用的筷子里充满哲理和智慧。

筷子不仅架起了人与食物之间的桥梁，同时也架起了人与人之间的桥梁。筷子不单单只是一副餐具，也可以作为礼物送与他人。过去，筷子常常作为姑娘的陪嫁品，意味着“筷子筷子，快生贵子”。朋友之间常以折筷盟誓，表示同心协力成就一番事业，或表示忠心耿耿等。十双筷子还有着十全十美、团团圆圆的意味。送商友筷子，寓意双木成林、合作长久。筷子早已是中国人生活中不可或缺的一部分。

筷子是中国人最主要的进餐工具，在使用时也有相应的一系列礼仪。餐桌前，孩子的人生第一课就是在父母的指导下学用筷子。宴请或聚餐时，用筷成为人们展示礼仪风范的一个窗口，筷起筷落之间，不可避免地透露着一个人的礼仪修养。用筷子有很多禁忌，比如忌讳用餐过程中筷子掉在地上，忌讳把筷子含在嘴里嘬并发出声音，忌讳把筷子插在米饭上递给对方，等等。仅仅通过一双小小的筷子就能够看出中国作为礼仪之邦所拥有的深厚的文化积淀。

筷子自古以来就寓意吉祥、安宁。一双筷子，方圆、笔直、齐整。孔子说："礼之用，和为贵。"中国人在餐桌上讲究用筷子只夹取自己面前的食物，不逾越到他人面前，这正是"和"为贵的表现。

SCAN FOR A VIDEO

Chapter 3
第三章

# Medicine as Food

# 美味的药

万象中国
CHINA BOUQUET
第二册
Book 2

# Medicine as Food

In 2003, archaeologists discovered a graveyard in Lop Nor, Xinjiang, and were marveled at the well-preserved mummies inside, one of which was a pretty female, affectionately known as "Xiaohe Princess". She had fair skin, a high-arched nose, and deep eyes with brown hair. She wore a felt cap with a bird's feather obliquely attached to its top. Around her waist was a basket containing a packet of ephedra, a herbal remedy for colds and other ailments, which proves that residents in Xiaohe began using ephedra as early as 3,500 years ago.

Many traditional Chinese medicines, such as ephedra, coptis root, and gentian root, taste bitter. Therefore, people looked for ways to make the medicine delicious, and Chinese medicinal cuisine is one such way.

People often believe that medicine and food are totally different, but both are highly homologous according to the theory and practices of TCM.

In ancient times, people had no permanent place to live or abundant food to select from. They sourced food from plants they picked, such as fruits, stems, leaves, and roots; animals they hunted, like cattle, sheep, pigs, and rabbits; and aquatic creatures they caught, such as fish, shells, and shrimps. An ancient Chinese legend tells of a farmer named Shennong (literally "Divine Farmer"), who tasted hundreds of herbs himself and was poisoned many times to test their efficacy. This is a typical example of the hardships Chinese ancestors once faced while hunting for food. Gradually, they discovered that croton results in diarrhea while pomegranate contains it; muskmelon base causes vomiting while ginger can stop it. Additionally, eating raw green beans can lead to poisoning, and consuming poisonous mushrooms can be fatal. Through numerous experiences and lessons, humans learned methods of identifying and selecting food. Over time, people discovered that some foods could ease ailments or even treat diseases. These accumulated experiences gradually helped people explore the universal principles of selecting food and medicine.

In their hunt for food, the ancient Chinese discovered that some medicines are edible while some foods possess medical effects. Food generally has fewer negative effects than medicine and can be used both to prevent and treat diseases, akin to medicine. The ancient pharmacists even identified the properties and functions of many foods and medicines, recognizing the difficulty in distinguishing between them because many foods and medicines served reciprocal functions. This elucidates the origin of the concept known as "the homology of food and medicine".

Wine and wheat koji were among the earliest substances to serve as both food and medicine. Most of the bronzes unearthed from Yin ruins in Henan Province, were wine vessels. At that time, people drank wine in daily life, used wine for sacrifices and treated diseases with it. Even the traditional Chinese character for "medicine" (醫) contains the component 酉, which originally meant a wine vessel and, by extension, the wine itself. Today, the tradition of using medicinal ingredients soaked in wine to cure diseases and maintain health still persists in China. Since wheat koji (called *maiqu* in Chinese) is a necessary ingredient for brewing wine, they are inseparable. The historical record indicates that the Chinese began using wheat koji to cure stomachaches as early as 59 BC. Over time, as its magical effect on promoting digestion was gradually discovered, *maiqu* was renamed *shenqu* (literally "magic wheat koji"), a term that is still in use today.

Based on the concept of the "homology of food and medicine", ancient medical scientists introduced a wide range of herbal medicines into daily cuisine recipes and invented "medicinal cuisine" to cure diseases and maintain health.

Zhou Yunhai, a medicinal cuisine chef, has been cooking medicinal food for 20 years. Every morning, he goes to pick fresh herbs to prepare for the day's feast. The greenhouse is full of verdant medicinal herbs, where Zhou picks some agastache rugosus, *sanqi*, and aloes. Agastache rugosus is an ideal medicinal diet in summer because it is conducive to releasing summer heat, relieving pain, and diarrhea. *Sanqi* can help promote blood circulation, dissipate stasis, and relieve swelling and pain. Aloes have the function of nurturing skins, so they are the optimal choice for women except pregnant ones.

To turn fresh medicinal herbs into delicious food, he needs not only the fresh ingredients, but also to combine them using the right recipe. Generally, the medicinal ingredients can be ingested as both food and medicine. The medical combinations must be measured in precise doses by doctors of traditional Chinese medicine before they are turned into food.

Having changed his overall, Zhou set out to cook. "*Sanqi* Leaves and Tofu Soup" requires a skillful chef. He needs to cut *sanqi* leaves and tofu into pieces as thin as human hair. Aloe by itself is sticky, bitter, and sour. But after being blanched, it becomes smooth and refreshing. Deep fried, it turns crisp on the outside and tender on the inside. This recipe calls for pouring tomato sauce over the aloe, giving it a delicious sweet and sour flavor. Agastache rugosus has a special flavor. After being steamed and then fried with chicken, it would still retain its nutritional and medicinal properties while having the perfect mixture of aroma and flavor.

The thoughtful combination of food and different medicinal ingredients, after stir-frying, frying, steaming, and stewing, can turn bitter-tasting medicine into delicious dishes. These dishes often win

acclaim from diners.

Zeng Wenyang, a TCM doctor, said, "From the beginning, traditional Chinese medicine has been considered homologous to food. The most famous prescription of TCM cuisine is called 'Guizhi Soup', and it is known as the ancestor of Chinese medicinal soup. It was invented by Yi Yin, a Shang Dynasty (1600-1046 BC) prime minister and also a renowned chef. Guizhi Soup uses cassia twig, Chinese peony, licorice, ginger, and dates. These five food ingredients are all considered common medicine and can be combined into a prescription."

Yi Yin was the earliest master chef in China and also served as a prime minister who assisted Cheng Tang in overthrowing the Xia Dynasty (2070-1600 BC) and establishing the Shang Dynasty. He helped Cheng Tang lay a solid foundation for the 600-year development of this dynasty. Legend has it that Yi Yin applied culinary philosophy to national governance, suggesting that governing a country is like cooking a small fish.

Yi Yin also invented the TCM soup. He was born along the Yishui River, which was abundant in herbal medicine. He was well-versed in both cooking and medicine. Through treating people's diseases, he discovered that the boiling herbal medicine proved to be more effective than using it raw. Therefore, to this day, medicinal soup remains one of the most common forms of TCM.

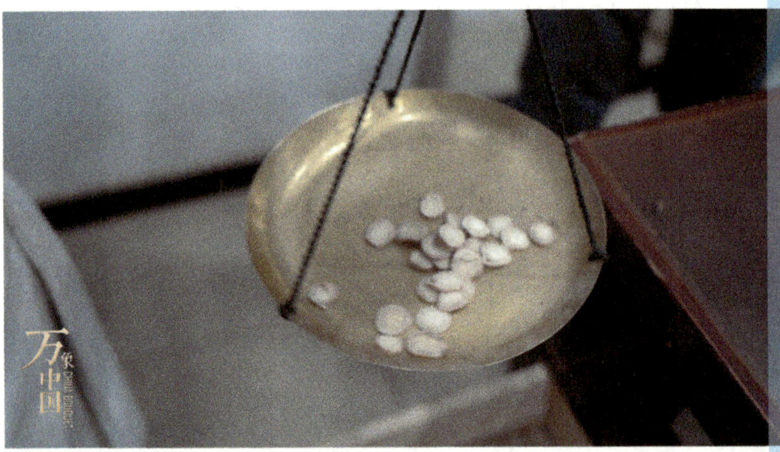

Yi Yin created a lot of herbal soups based on his experiences in treating diseases and culinary techniques. Guizhi Soup is a typical example, made of various spices, including cassia twigs, ginger, and dates, which remain common spices in our kitchens today. Therefore, some scholars even claim that Guizhi Soup is the preferred choice for

food therapy.

Zeng Wenyang said, "Since the beginning, traditional Chinese medicine has been considered homologous to food. It has undergone millennia of research and development, spanning all the dynasties in Chinese history. For instance, in the seventh century, the medical monograph *Shi Liao Ben Cao* (*Materia Medica of Diet Therapy*) detailed the relationship between food and medicinal ingredients."

Chinese people believe that the human body is closely related to everything in the world. The laws of nature and the harmony between humans and nature are what Chinese people strive to follow throughout their lifetime.

In the past 5,000 years, Chinese people have accumulated profound food culture. Based on traditional Chinese medicine, a unique medicinal food culture was formed. Chinese medicinal food has become a part of modern life.

The medicinal cuisine is based on the prescription of herbs and the selection of dishes. It takes delicacy as the keynote and health as the purpose to nourish the body and mind of the Chinese people.

# 美味的药

2003年，在中国新疆罗布泊，考古学家发现了一片墓地。墓中大量保存完好的干尸引起考古学家的惊叹，其中有一位女性尤以美貌著称，她白肤栗发，高鼻深目，头戴尖顶毡帽，帽顶斜插着鸟的羽毛，人称“小河公主”。小河公主的腰间用小筐装着一包麻黄——一种中国的草药，可治疗风寒感冒等病症。这说明在3500年前小河居民就会使用麻黄了。

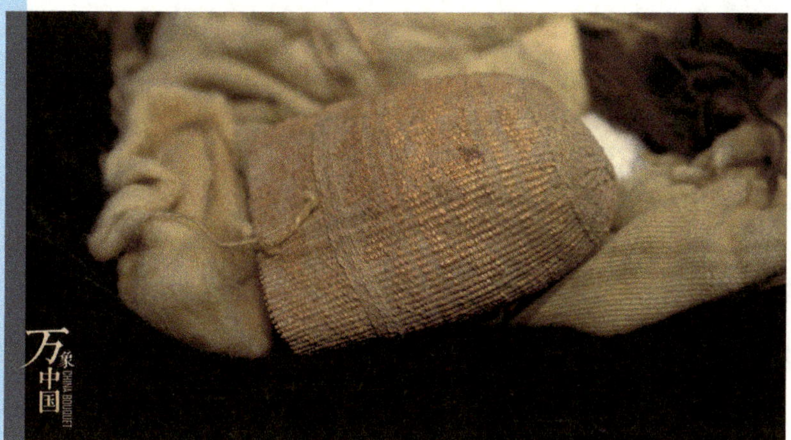

麻黄、黄连、龙胆草等很多中药味苦，难以下咽，所以古代人便开始琢磨怎样将苦苦的药材变得好吃，药膳就是一种方式。

在一般人的观念里，药物和食物是完全不同并被严格区分的两类物质，可是在中医药学理论和实践中，它们却具有高度的同源性。

在远古时代，人们居无定所、饥不择食，食物来源于采摘收集的果实、茎叶、根块等植物，来源于狩猎而得的牛、羊、猪、兔等动物，还有的来源于捕捞所获的鱼类、贝类、虾类等水生动物。“神农尝百草”的传说就反映了中国的祖先寻找食物的艰辛。慢慢地，人们发现：吃了巴豆会拉肚子，吃了石榴能够止泻；吃了甜瓜瓜蒂会呕吐，吃了生姜能够止呕；吃了生扁豆会中毒，吃了毒蘑菇会丧命……无数次经验和教训的积累，让人类学到了辨别和选择食物的方法。后来，人们又发现了有些食物能够缓解身体的不适，还能够治疗某些病痛。随着经验的积累，人们渐渐地摸索出充饥的食物与治病的药物的一般应用规律。

古人在寻找食物的过程中发现，有些药物是食物，而有些食物也是药物；食物的不良反应小，而药物的不良反应大；食物和药物同样能够防治疾病。古代医家们还发现了各种食物和药物的性味和功效，认识到许多食物可以药用，许多药物也可以食用，两者之间很难严格区分。这就是中医“药食同源”的由来。

酒和麦曲可能是最早的既作为食物也作为药物使用的东西。从殷墟发掘出来的青铜器大多为酒器，那时候的人们日常饮酒，祭祀用酒，治病也用酒，甚至繁体汉字“醫”中就已经包含了酒的语义——“酉”的本义是酒器，引申为酒。现在中国人还有用酒泡药材治病养生的传统。因为酿酒要用曲，所以酒和曲是分不开的。史载公元前59年中国人就开始用麦曲治胃病，后来慢慢发现用麦曲治消化不良有神效，故把麦曲命名为“神曲”，至今在生活中依然常用。

基于“药食同源”的思想，古代医学家将许多药物广泛用于日常饮食之中，还发明了“药膳”用来治病和养生。

周云海是一位药膳厨师，做药膳有20年了。每天一早，他就要去采摘新鲜的药材，为了让即将迎来的食客们大快朵颐做准

备。种植大棚里面种满了翠绿的药材，周师傅采摘了一些藿香和三七，砍了几根芦荟。藿香用于解暑散热、止痛止泻，非常适合夏天吃，三七具有活血化瘀、消肿定痛的作用，而芦荟是美容养颜的佳品，非常适合女性食用，但是孕妇除外。

要把新鲜的药材制作成美味的食物，除了要采摘最新鲜的草药外，还要搭配好菜品，一般选用的药材都是“药食同源”的，即可用作菜品又可入药，这需要经过中医进行合理搭配，精确掌控用量。

周师傅换上工作服，开始做菜了。银丝藤三七汤很考验刀工，三七的叶子和豆腐都要切成如发丝一般粗细。芦荟本身黏腻

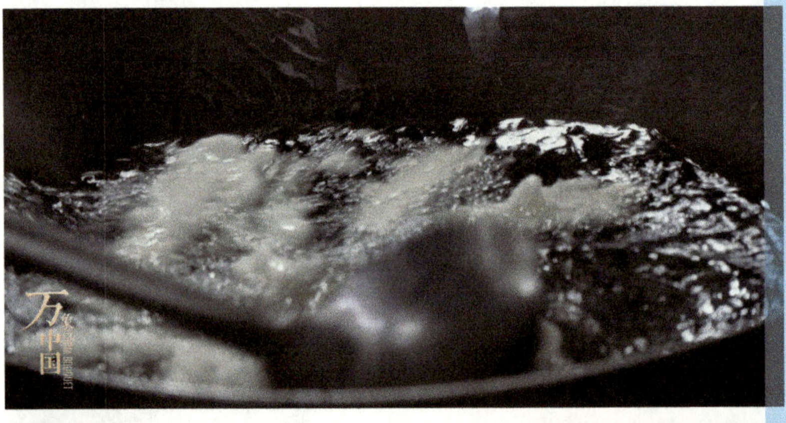

酸涩，而经过过水处理就会滑嫩爽口，油炸后的口感外酥里嫩，浇上番茄汁则酸甜可口。藿香本身有特殊的味道，经过先蒸后炸可以保留营养与药物的功效，藿香白玉鸡这道菜中的藿香就与鸡肉的香气完美地融合在了一起。

不同食材与药材进行搭配，经过煎炒烹炸蒸炖，原本难以下咽的药物就变成了美味的菜肴。这样的一席菜常常赢得食客的点头称赞。

中医曾文暘说："中医最早就是从药食同源开始的。最著名、最经典的方剂叫'桂枝汤'，这个方被称为群方之祖，是由商朝的宰相伊尹发明的，他同时也是一位厨师。'桂枝汤'里面用的药有桂枝、芍药、甘草、生姜与大枣，这五味药也是常见的食材，将这几种食材拼在一起就成为了一种方剂。"

伊尹是中国最早的烹饪大师，同时，他又作为商朝辅国宰相助成汤灭夏，建立商朝，辅佐成汤奠定了商朝600年的基业。相传，他将烹饪理论与治国之道结合起来，提出了"治大国如烹小鲜"的道理。

伊尹还是中药汤剂的发明者。伊尹出生于草药丰富的伊水流域，既善于烹调，又精通医学。在为百姓治病的过程中，他总结出一个经验：将草药煮熟服下比生食效果要好。因此至今，汤液仍然是中国人服用中药的一种最常用的形态。

伊尹总结草药治病的经验，再结合烹调技术，创制了许多汤方。桂枝汤就是用辛香调味料创制的。其中的桂、姜、枣至今仍是我们厨房里的常用调料。因此，有学者称桂枝汤为“食疗之首”。

曾文暘说：“中医的开始其实就是药食同源，随后历朝历代都在不断推陈出新，比如说唐朝的《食疗本草》就很详细地介绍了食物跟药材之间的关系。”

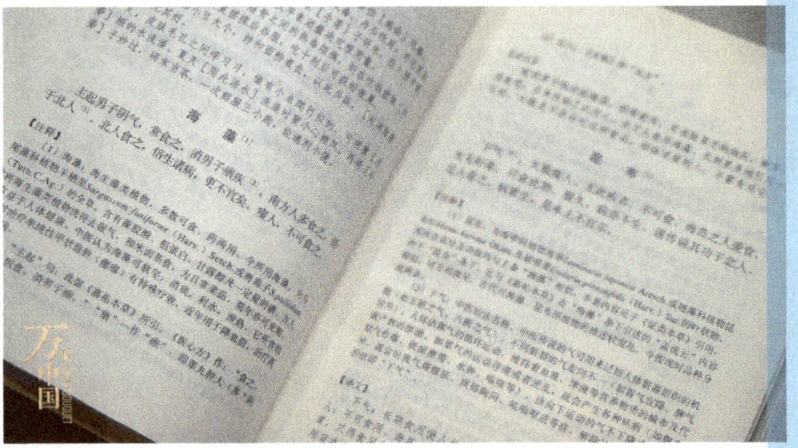

中国人认为身体与大千世界的万事万物之间息息相关，“天人合一”与“道法自然”的生命认知贯穿于中国人的思维中。

五千年的岁月积淀出了中国深厚的饮食文化底蕴，在中医理论的基础上又形成了独具特色的药膳文化。药膳已经成为了现代生活的一部分。

药膳以美味为基调，以健康为目的，遣药为方，选材成肴，滋养着中国人的身心。

SCAN FOR A VIDEO

Chapter 4
第四章

# She's Silk
# 一抹丝绸

万象中国
CHINA BOUQUET

第二册
Book 2

# She's Silk

One day in 3000 BC, while the Yellow Emperor's wife, Leizu, was sitting in the mulberry forest drinking, a cocoon fell into her tea from a tree. A long, thin silk thread appeared as she took the cocoon out.

This romantic imagination of silk's origin from folklore illustrates the long history of silk in China. China was the earliest country to raise silkworms and produce silk, enjoying the advantage of being the only country capable of doing so for an extended period.

The silk threads, silk bands, and plain silk pieces excavated from Archaeological Ruins of Liangzhu City in 1958 are the earliest silk artifacts along the lower reaches of the Yangtze River, dating back over 4,700 years ago. In the Shang Dynasty (1600-1046 BC), people could produce silk with flower patterns and exquisite embroidery. Silk production gradually evolved into a national industry, bringing about prosperity over centuries. In the Zhou Dynasty (1046-256 BC), comprehensive development was made in silkworm cultivation, mulberry cultivation, and silk fabric production, as recorded in the anthology *Classic of Poetry*. One of the poems, "Bin Feng", in the anthology provides a detailed description, including planting mulberry, rearing silkworm, reeling silk, weaving, dyeing, and making clothes.

In the Han Dynasty (206 BC-AD 220), the silkworm industry spread wider into the Hexi Corridor region, with Shu Embroidery in Chengdu enjoying a great reputation. In 200 BC, Emperor Wudi of the Han Dynasty dispatched the envoy Zhang Qian for a westward expedition, pioneering the Silk Road, which is well-known worldwide. Additionally, the purchase of silk fabric by a large number of Western commercial fleets further facilitated the production of silk fabric, resulting in the first pinnacle of silk production in China's history. Since then, China's silk has begun to be introduced to the West, with camel bells resonating in the desert.

Westerners highly favored China's silk. The long silk robe from China that the Roman Empire's Caesar wore to watch a play won the audience's admiration, making Caesar the "marketer" of China's silk. The royal families and noblemen in ancient Greece and Rome took pride in their silk garments. Constantinople, located at the end of the Silk Road, required a significant amount of labor, funds, and physical support to ship silk; therefore, the price of silk could be as high as that of gold. Historical documents record that 450 grams of silk could cost as much as 600 grams of gold. Silk was regarded as soft gold. Ancient Roman officials even considered silk to be a symbol of fortune and power, and they were willing to exchange a silk garment for one year's salary.

The second peak of silk production occurred during the Tang and Song dynasties. The silk from the Tang Dynasty (618-907) was as transparent as ice. An Arab merchant, wealthy and curious, encountered an official selecting products for the royal court in Guangzhou. Upon noticing the merchant's gaze fixed upon his chest, the official inquired about the reason. The merchant responded, "Although you wear two silk garments, I can still see the black moles on your chest." The official smiled and said, "Actually, I wear five garments, not just two." Rendered speechless, the merchant then commented, "The finest silk is the raw silk that hasn't been bleached. The silk you are wearing looks even more beautiful." He further noted, "Without the royal court's approval, the silk cannot be exported to Arab countries. Should it be sold there, the price would be exorbitant." This anecdotes illustrates that the silk products from the Tang Dynasty were both exquisite and expensive, enjoying widespread popularity around the globe.

About 4,700 years ago, silkworm rearing, silk reeling and weaving had already emerged and been widely developed in Taihu Lake Basin in Suzhou, China. The region later became famous for its people's delicate and exquisite lifestyle. The delicate silk fabric needs people's long-term effort, and it is also a product that can only be achieved by a dedicated design and skillful handcraft.

During the Song Dynasty (960-1279), numerous private silk workshops emerged, producing a variety of silk products to promote the prosperity of the silk trade. Since the Song Dynasty, Suzhou has been the hub of China's silk industry, producing excellent silk products. To this day, Suzhou remains the center of silk production, with hand looms still in operation there.

Huang Yunying is weaving a twisted warp silk fabric called *luo* together with another experienced silk weaver. The technique used to produce *luo* is swivel weaving. Even with modern technologies and equipment, the patterned silk and the four-warp twisted silk, with their delicate texture, exquisite craftsmanship, and intricate decorative patterns, can only be produced by hand using a large string-heddle patterning loom. The pattern to be woven would be designed and coded into a pattern format. The shuttle-picking and jacquard workers must

work together to pull and draw threads, press tappet, pick shuttles, and so on. Singing folk songs is also a big part of the weaving process. Huang Yunying is fully occupied with the silk thread in her hand. She knows every single thread has its own route and cannot have any deviations. Accuracy, stability, and patience are crucial traits for an experienced weaver.

Huang Yunying says, "I have been in the silk industry for more than two decades. Whenever I receive a new pattern or fabric, I look forward to a better product. I hope the whole world can appreciate our silk. It is my wish."

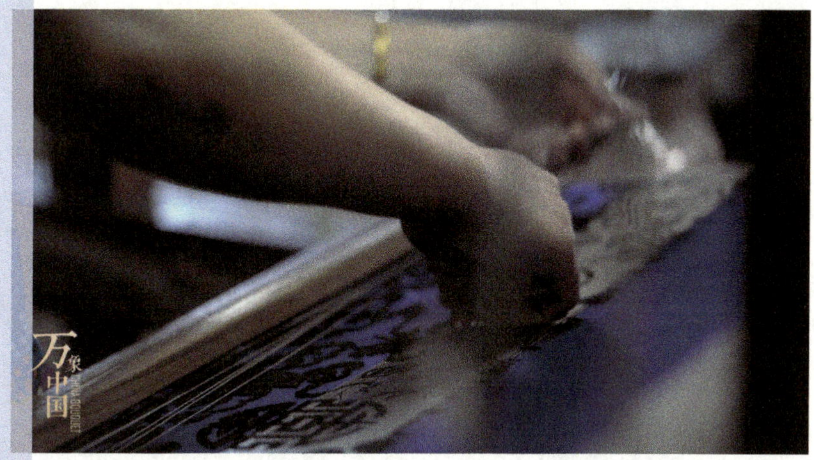

What kind of magical insects enables Chinese people to weave such exquisite silk products? Silkworm. It originated in China and undergoes four stages: egg, larva, pupa, adult moth. The threads that the silkworm spits out are the best, longest, and thinnest textile fibers among all natural fibers.

In the region south of the Yangtze River, the silkworm nursery is filled with shelves in spring, each of which is scattered with shallow baskets. The baskets are covered with mulberry leaves inside, with baby silkworms lying on them. While the silkworms are silently eating the fresh and tender mulberry leaves, the entire nursery resonates with the rustling sound of chewing and swallowing. The baby silkworms, fed with mulberry leaves, are spinning silk. After two weeks, they will be tightly wrapped in silk, looking like little snowballs.

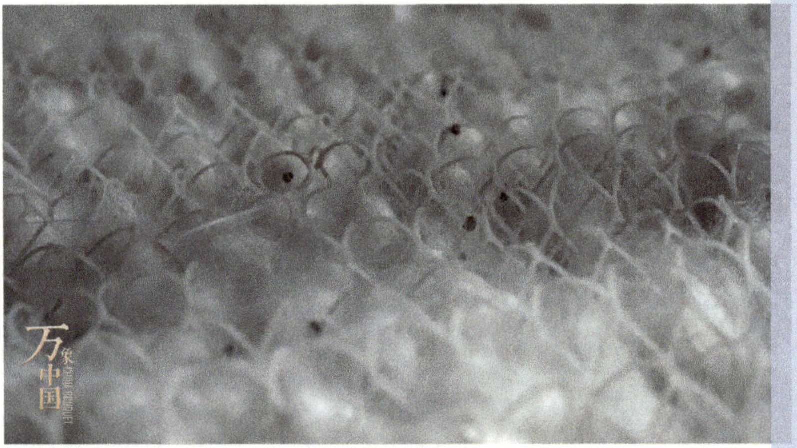

A single cocoon could produce more than 1,000 meters of silk threads. Weavers would draw and reel silk threads from cocoons and then weave them into marvelous silk fabric.

In China, silk has always been an expensive and precious material for exquisite garments. Chinese people, especially women, are very fond of silk.

Chu Yan is a fashion designer born in Xi'an. She is doing the final preparations for her upcoming fashion show. For her, silk is more than just a fabric. It not only connects all craftsmen from ancient times to the present but inherits and carries on the nation's greatest aesthetic imaginations as well.

Chu Yan says, "When we look back at traditional Chinese clothing and fabrics, we can find the most exquisite weaving, the most beautiful colors, and the most complicated embroidery patterns on silk fabrics. Before industrial production, silk was a rare material. Perhaps because it was too precious for ordinary garments, people would always try their best to weave the silk into exquisite fabrics with auspicious and beautiful patterns."

Because of her passion for silk, Chu Yan has been exploring how to sustain the development of traditional costume culture by combining it with modern design and ways of life.

In May, 2023, the China-Central Asia Summit was held in Xi'an, where leaders from different countries gathered wearing traditional Chinese costumes. Chu Yan and her team designed these costumes. Chu tried to make the costumes look more graceful and resplendent by integrating numerous elements regarding Xi'an and Silk Road and using multiple of China's non-intangible cultural heritage techniques, such as Su Embroidery and *Wuluo*, displaying to the world the ancient charm of China over the past thousands of years.

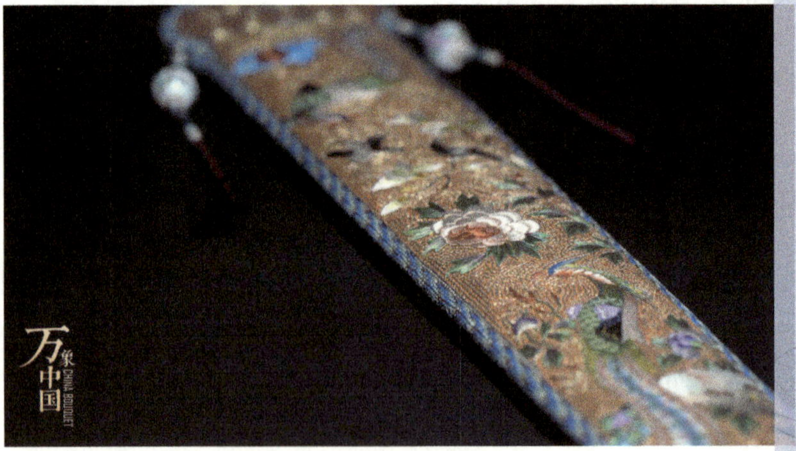

Passed down in clothing, silk suggests a kind of moderation and softness, which are valued in Confucian culture.

Since the beginning of the Silk Road, silk has become a symbol of Chinese etiquette and culture. It is an expression of peace and friendship, like flowing water and moving clouds that never stop. It will spread across the world, bringing people beauty and elegance.

Every nation has its own unique and precious treasures. For the Chinese people, silk is one of them. Silk always shines wherever it is. When feeling the soft and smooth silk, who won't fall in love with it?

# 一抹丝绸

公元前3000年的一天，黄帝的妻子西陵氏坐在桑林喝茶，当时一个蚕茧从树上落到她的茶水中，她取出蚕茧，一根纤细的长丝线就出来了……

这是一个浪漫的民间传说，从中可以看出中国丝绸有着悠久的历史。中国是世界上最早饲养家蚕和织造丝绸的国家，并且在相当长的时期内是唯一一个懂养蚕织丝的国家。

1958年，在良渚文化遗址中出土了距今4700多年前的桑蚕丝线、丝带和平纹绢片，这是中国长江下游地区出土的年代最早的丝绸实物。到了商代，人们已经能织造带暗花的绸子并带有绚丽的刺绣，丝绸生产变成全国性的产业并带来千百年的繁荣。周代，蚕、桑、丝织全面发展，《诗经》中有许多对蚕桑丝织生产的表述，《豳风·七月》描述得尤为具体全面，几乎包括了种桑、养蚕、缫丝、纺织、染色、成衣的全过程。

到了汉代，蚕桑丝织生产的地域有了扩展，蚕桑业已经传入河西走廊，成都的蜀锦驰名天下。公元前2世纪，汉武帝派张骞出使西域，开辟了举世闻名的“丝绸之路”。大批西方商队来到中国采购丝绸，这也进一步促进了丝绸的生产，汉代是中国历史上丝绸生产的第一个高峰期。从此，中国的丝绸源源不断地流向西方，漫漫黄沙上的驼铃声不绝于耳。

中国的丝绸在西方受到难以想象的喜爱。古罗马的凯撒大帝曾穿着中国丝绸长袍去看戏，引起全场的钦羡。凯撒大帝以一己之力成了丝绸的“带货王”，古希腊和古罗马的皇室、贵族都以拥有丝绸服饰而自豪。由于君士坦丁堡处于丝绸之路的末端，丝绸运到那里需要花费巨大的人力、物力和财力，以至于丝绸的价格堪比黄金，有史料记载，在当地，9两丝绸的价格是12两黄金，可以说丝绸是名副其实的软黄金。古罗马官员视丝绸为富贵与权势的象征，愿意以一年的工资来换取一件丝绸服装。

唐宋时期是中国丝绸生产的第二个高峰期。唐代的绢透明似冰。当时，一位阿拉伯富商在广州拜会一位为宫廷选货的官员。

商人老盯着官员的胸口，官员问其何故。商人说：“你虽然穿了两件绸衣，但我还能看到你胸口上的黑痣。”官员听后大笑，说：“我穿的不是两件，而是五件。”商人瞠目结舌，说：“最好的丝绸是未经漂白的生丝。您穿的这种丝绸比生丝更美、更出色。”商人还说：“这种丝绸，因为没有取得朝廷的许可，还不能运到阿拉伯各国去，而且要价高得没个谱。”这一故事生动地反映了唐代绢织品的精美和昂贵，及其在世界上受欢迎的程度。

4700年前，中国苏州的太湖流域已有养蚕、取丝和织红的传统。在这片后来以江南精致细腻生活方式著称的地区，娇美的丝绸是人们悉心看顾和心手合一的产物。

宋代民间出现了很多独立的私人丝织作坊，它们生产各种丝织品，促进了丝绸贸易的繁荣。自宋朝以来，苏州一直是中国丝织业的中心，这里所产的丝织品光彩夺目。直到今天，苏州依然是丝绸的重要产地，依然保留着人工织机。

丝绸织造师黄云英正和另一位有经验的织工一起利用挖花工艺织造一种真丝的绞经织物——“罗”。即使在科技和工业文明高度发达的今天，质地精密、工艺考究、纹饰精美的妆花和四经绞罗依然要依靠传统的大花楼木织机与人的配合才能完成。要织造的图案经由设计和编码成为“提花本”，投梭工与挽花工相互配合：拉牵、踏综、投梭、串综打纬，边唱边织。黄云英全神贯注于手中的丝线，串综打纬，一丝一缕都不能错过。对一名训练有素的织造师来说，眼准、手稳、耐心缺一不可。

黄云英说：“我做了二十几年的丝绸了，每次都期待接下来有什么单子，有什么新的面料我们能把它做得更成功一点，让世

界各地的人们都认可我们织的这些品种。我一直有这种想法。”

是怎样神奇的虫子让中国人可以织出如此精美的丝绸呢？蚕，原产于中国，一生中要经过卵、幼虫、蛹、成虫四个发育阶段。蚕吐出的丝是所有天然纤维中最优良、最绵长、最纤细的纺织纤维。

春天，江南的蚕室摆满了架子，每一层上都布满笸箩，里面铺满桑叶，桑叶上趴着一层蚕宝宝。春天的桑叶鲜嫩可口，蚕宝宝趴在上面静静地吃着桑叶，整个蚕室充满了“沙沙”的声音，那是蚕在咀嚼吞咽。吃饱了桑叶的蚕宝宝开始成长，长大后开始吐丝。两周后，它们吐出的丝会将自己紧紧包裹，成为一个个小“雪球”。

一颗普通的蚕茧可以抽出上千米的蚕丝。人们抽丝剥茧，缫丝成线，经过在织机上无数个日夜的织造，丝绸才能诞生。

在中国，丝绸被视为一种十分贵重的服饰面料。中国人，尤其是女性，对它无比喜爱。

出生于西安市的服装设计师楚艳正在为其新一季的服装大秀

进行着最后的准备工作。对她来说，丝绸不仅是一种面料，它连接着古往今来所有的能工巧匠，承继着中华民族对美的全部想象。

楚艳说：“在中国传统的服饰或传统的织物中，那最精湛的织造技艺、最漂亮的颜色、最复杂的刺绣图案都是用在丝绸面料上的。中国古代不是一个工业化的时代，不是一个大机器生产的时代，所以它（丝绸）一直是最为珍稀的制衣原料。古人大概是觉得丝绸太稀有了，所以一定要把它织成一个非常美的、有着各种漂亮吉祥纹样的服饰或织物。”

出于对丝绸的热爱，楚艳一直在探索传统服饰文化如何与当代时尚设计相结合、与当代生活方式相结合，由此赋予传统服饰文化可持续发展的生命力。

2023年5月，中国—中亚峰会在西安市举行，各国领导人穿着主办国的传统服装亮相，这些服装就是楚艳和她的团队设计的。楚艳在服装上应用了大量西安和丝路美学元素，以及多项中国非遗传统技艺，比如苏绣、吴罗，使服装尽显雍容富丽的唐风雅韵，向世界展现了千年古国的时代风貌。

丝绸，借助于人、机杼，传承于服饰，植根于中国五千年的文化底蕴。丝绸以它的丝滑和柔韧从另一个角度诠释了儒家文化的“中庸”思想。

自丝绸之路开始，丝绸便承载着中国的礼仪与文化，象征着和平与友谊，如“行云流水”，延绵不绝地散播向世界各地，给各国人民带去别样的美丽与高贵。

丝绸，始终是中国人情有独钟的所在，总是世人目光汇聚的焦点。当丝绸温柔地在你的肌肤上流动，谁又能不爱上它呢。

SCAN FOR A VIDEO

Chapter 5
第五章

# Traditional Chinese Makeup

# 红妆悦己

万象中国
第二册
Book 2

# Traditional Chinese Makeup

In ancient China, the color used most often in women's makeup was red, and that was how the traditional makeup style *hongzhuang* (red makeup) earned its name. With today's popularity of Chinese fashion, more and more young people are honoring traditions and culture with various styles of makeup and clothing, and one of the ways is through "red makeup".

Wang Aonan, a makeup artist, is a disciple of a master of Chinese traditional makeup Yang Shuyun. She told me the reason why she chose this profession, "When I was a child, I watched a lot of TV series, like *Dream of Red Mansions* and *The Legend of White Snake*. I would wear sheets as costumes and put on my mother's lipstick, dressing myself like a heroine in the TV series. It was not until college that I began wearing traditional Chinese makeup. Later, I was introduced by my friend to my teacher, Mr. Yang Shuyun. Professionally, he taught me how to put on the red makeup.

"My personal favorite is the makeup style from the Tang Dynasty (618-907), which is diverse and magnificent. I think my personal style is more in line with that. When I wear my *Hanfu* robes and put on traditional makeup, it feels like that my childhood dream of becoming a fairy princess has finally come true."

Yang Shuyun has been engaged in the film and stage makeup career for over 50 years, contributing significantly to the development of screen styling in China. He is well-known for his designs of ancient and historical characters on screen, hailed as "the first designer of historical characters".

Yang is well-versed in stage makeup and costume design. He was responsible for designing the makeup and styling for the dance drama *Silu Huayu*, which debuted in 1979. This drama received a strong reaction worldwide.

In 1986, Yang Shuyun served as the makeup designer for the TV series *Dream of Red Mansions*, helping vividly display the beauty of the twelve ancient Chinese ladies depicted in the novel of the same name written by Cao Xueqin. These portrayals left a deep impression on audiences. Although several decades have passed, Lin Daiyu's delicate eyebrows, childish small plaits, and the varied hair buns and hair ornaments as the plot changes continue to resonate in the minds of the audience. People believe she is a fairy from the Great Illusion Realm and Sister Lin "descending from Heaven". Yang's input and wisdom are embedded in the widely acknowledged masterpiece, the TV series *Dream of Red Mansions* (1987 Edition).

Afterward, Yang Shuyun provided makeup and hairstyling for TV series such as *Emperor Xuanzong of Tang* and *Hymn of Zhenguan* as well as the film *Concubine Yang*, all of which have won major awards.

Yang Shuyun said, "There are ancient records of Chinese women wearing makeup. According to the *Admonitions Scroll*, the makeup concept was put forward in the fourth century. Chinese women in ancient times were believed to have ignored three-dimensional shading when applying makeup. In truth, from the Tang Dynasty style called 'three white spaces', we can find proof that Chinese ladies of that period had already begun to wear three-dimensional makeup on their faces."

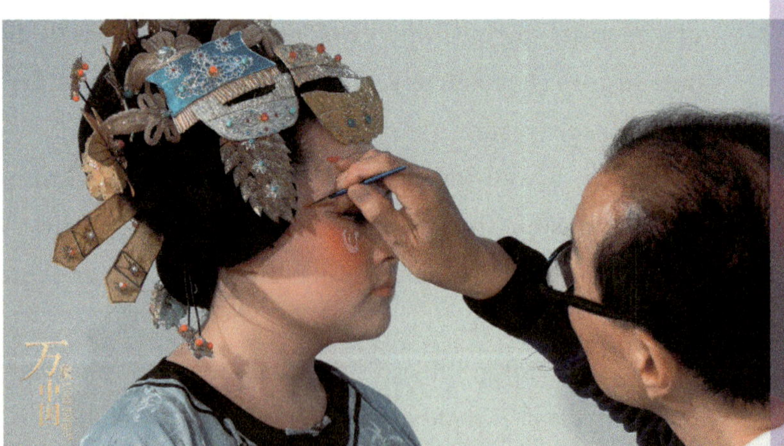

The Tang Dynasty is the pinnacle in the history of makeup in China. The prosperous era brought openness and boldness to society, leading to the exaggeration and exquisiteness of female makeup.

Hairstyles are a typical example featuring an exaggerated design style. In the Tang Dynasty, a symbolic change was the looser arched sideburns and a lowered hair bun in the front of the head top, which was the most popular hairstyle at that time, spreading across China.

In the prime of the Tang Dynasty, women often used rouge to apply red makeup to their faces. It looked so exaggerated because the entire face was covered with heavy rouge except for the forehead, nose bridge, and jaw. Legend has it that Concubine Yang was so sorrowful when bidding farewell to her parents that she shed tears. As she was about to set off, the cold weather made the tears on her face freeze into red thin ice. The red makeup during this period can be considered the heaviest makeup.

There are many descriptions of the red makeup worn by women in the Tang Dynasty. The Tang Dynasty poet Li Bai once described a lady in Yexi with a face as white as jade, green eyebrows, and red makeup. The other Tang poet, Cen Shen, commented in his poem that wearing red makeup was the most beautiful moment for a woman.

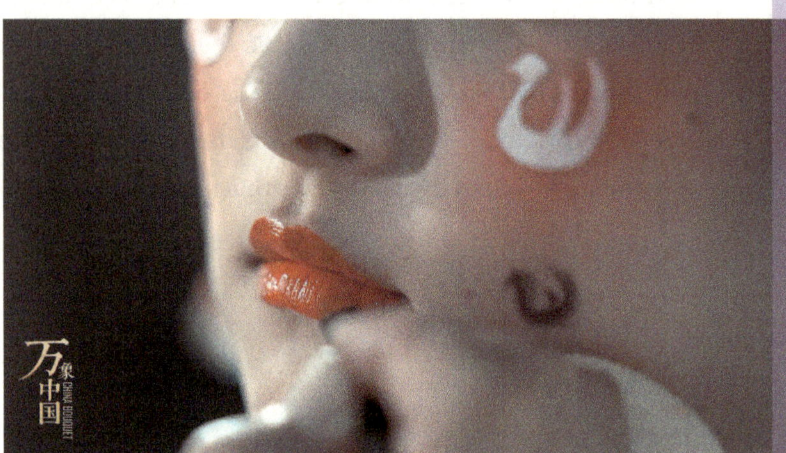

*The Anecdotes of Kaiyuan and Tianbao Periods* recorded that the red powders on Concubine Yang's face even reddened her sweat. Another Tang poet, Wang Jian, in his work *Palace Poems* even recounted that the water left in the basin by a court lady after washing her face seemed like red clay.

Meanwhile, exquisite and gorgeous makeup gradually gained

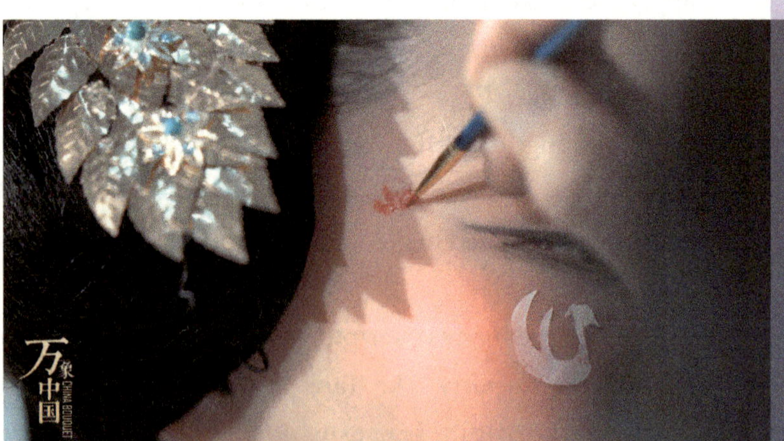

popularity, with flower patterns growing on women's faces. Typical makeup styles like *xiehong*, *ehuang*, and *jiaye* appeared on women's faces.

At that time, most of the noblewomen in the capital, Chang'an, wore refined and delicate makeup, featuring swollen sideburns and lowered hair buns. They were attired in flower-patterned dresses, presenting a plump figure.

Nowadays, with the improvement of Chinese people's lives, their pursuit of cultural activities has become more diversified. Many young people have fallen in love with ancient makeup and hairstyling; as a result, they all want to have a hands-on experience, leading to a surge in the pursuit of the ancient makeup style.

Wang Aonan said, "Before I came to Chengdu, I had other jobs, but then I quit them to focus on traditional makeup. Now, I run an online store selling products related to *Hanfu* and teach girls to wear classical makeup. I appreciate the red makeup as it has helped me to discover a better life. It's often said that a girl will doll herself up for he who appreciates her, but I think girls wear makeup to find their better selves. When I was a child, I yearned to wear makeup in the classic style. I have finally realized my dream."

While makeup styles change all the time, women's love of beauty has remained the same. The beauty of the East is not only graceful and restrained but as gorgeous and bright as the makeup of the Tang Dynasty. Girls back then were bold and outgoing. Their free and independent attitude towards life embodies the inclusiveness and development of Chinese culture. Beauty does not only come from wearing makeup. It also comes from your confidence and wisdom. "Red makeup" decorates the girls' faces, illustrating their yearning and pursuit of a better life. Nowadays, in addition to showcasing one's personality, a woman's choice in makeup and accessories is also a way to express herself and her attitudes towards the outside world. What they care about the most is no longer being solely focused on by men but rather their own way of expressing beauty. In the past, girls wore makeup to please men, but now they can find their own joy in wearing makeup, which is an example that demonstrates the progress of society.

# 红妆悦己

在中国古代，女子的妆饰多用到红色，因此这种传统妆容被称为“红妆”。随着国潮的流行，越来越多的中国年轻人以不同的方式把古代妆容画在脸上，穿在身上，刻在心里。红妆就是其中之一。

王傲男是一位化妆师，师从中国古典妆造大师杨树云。之所以选择这行，她说：“我小时候经常看电视剧，像《红楼

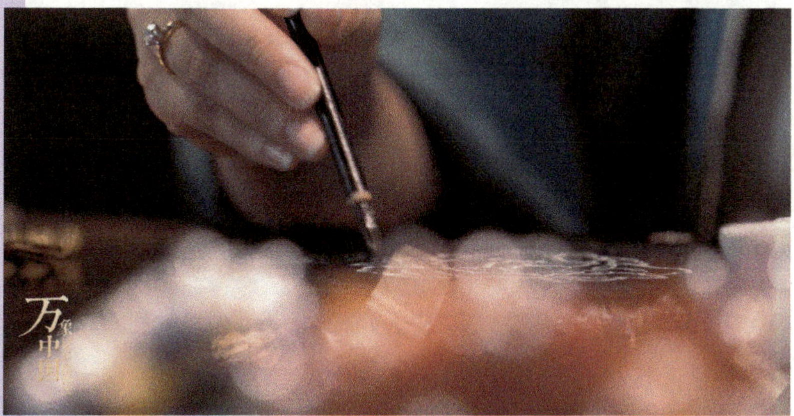

梦》《新白娘子传奇》，我们女孩子会披着床单，偷用妈妈的口红，打扮成电视剧里女主人公的样子。后来上大学的时候，我开始接触中国复古妆容，直到我的朋友把我引荐给杨树云老师，我才开始真正系统地学习古妆。”

“我最喜欢的还是唐代的妆容，它多变而且大气磅礴，我个人觉得自己的形象也更符合唐妆。当穿上汉服、画上古代妆容之后，我觉得自己小时候‘变成仙女’的梦想仿佛真的实现了。”

杨树云老师从事影视舞台化妆事业50多年，为中国影视造型的发展做出过卓越的贡献，在业界以整体塑造古代造型著称，有“天下第一梳”之美誉。

在舞台化妆造型领域，杨树云具有很深的造诣，1979年首次上演的著名舞剧《丝路花雨》的化妆造型就是由他设计的，当时在全世界引起了强烈的反响。

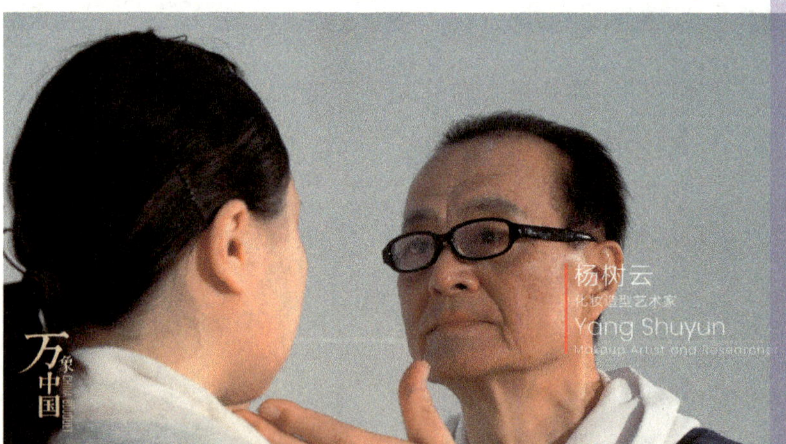


1986年，杨树云担任电视剧《红楼梦》的化妆设计。他完美演绎了曹雪芹原著《红楼梦》中以金陵十二钗为代表的中国

古代人物造型，给观众留下了深刻的印象。几十年过去了，林黛玉那让人怜爱的罥烟眉，那几根充满童真的小辫子，那随着剧情的发展而变换的发髻和钗环，都深深印在了观众的脑海中，人们认定她就是那个太虚幻境中的绛珠仙子、“天上掉下的林妹妹”。87版电视剧《红楼梦》被公认为经典剧目，这其中也凝聚了杨树云的心血和智慧。

此后，杨树云还为电视剧《唐明皇》《贞观长歌》、电影《杨贵妃》等影视剧做过化妆造型，均获大奖。

杨树云说：“中国有悠久的梳妆文化传统，从公元4世纪的绘画作品《女史箴图》可以看出，那时中国就已经提出了‘美容’的理念。原来世人都以为中国的女人不讲究立体，实际上，我们通过中国古画中的三白画法可以看到，一千多年以前的唐代已经非常注重女性立体的美了。”

唐代是中国化妆史上最辉煌的时代。开元盛世给整个社会带来了开放、豪迈的气息，女性的妆容也向夸张和精致化发展。

夸张的首要表现就是发型。唐代最具符号性的改变就是隆起的半圈鬓发越发蓬松，头顶小髻前移低垂，这种发型作为当时最流行的发型传遍全国。

在繁华的唐朝，女子用胭脂化自己喜欢的“红妆”，即在涂上白粉之后，整个脸部都涂上浓重的红色胭脂，范围甚至从眉下一直蔓延到耳窝、眼角，全脸只剩下额头、鼻梁和下巴露白，相当夸张。传说杨贵妃在和双亲告别的时候悲痛得泪水滴落，等到上车启程的时候，因为外面的天气比较寒冷，她脸上的泪水竟然被冻成了红色的薄冰。历代红妆浓淡深浅不同，盛唐时代的这种大面积红妆可能是最浓烈的一种。

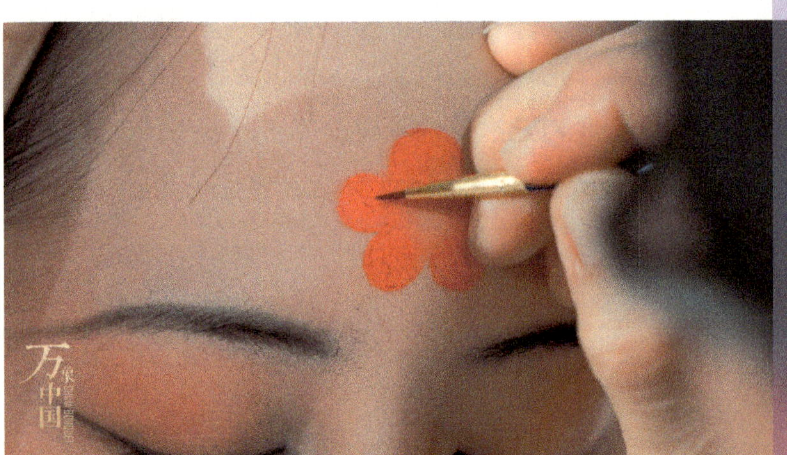

有关唐代妇女饰红妆的描绘有很多：李白的“玉面耶溪女，青蛾红粉妆”；岑参的“美人红妆色正鲜”；《开元天宝遗事》中记载，杨贵妃因为涂抹了红粉，连汗水都染成了红色；王建《宫词》中“归到院中重洗面，金花盆里泼红泥”，相传宫女洗脸后盆中水如红泥一般，可能是真实的写照。

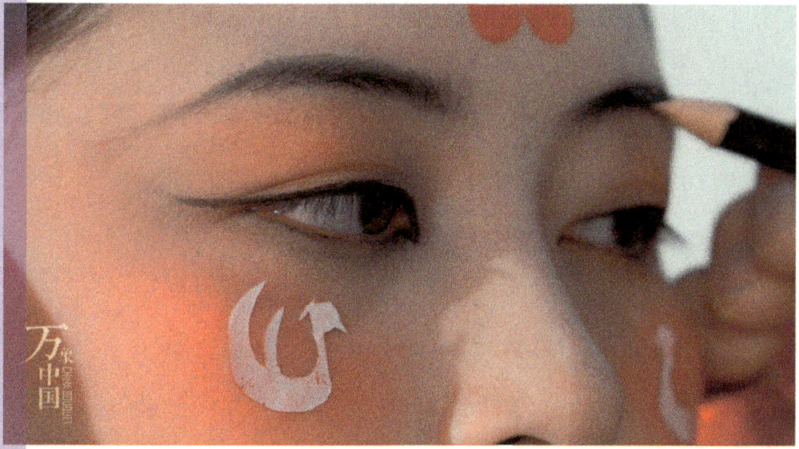

与此同时，精致华丽的妆饰也逐渐流行，女性脸上的花饰增多，典型的斜红、额黄、假靥等全套妆面也出现在女性的脸上。

当时长安城中的贵妇们大都梳着隆起的鬟发、低垂的小髻，画着精致柔美的妆容，穿着缀有花饰的衣裙，且身材日渐丰满。

现在，中国人的生活越来越好了，精神追求也多样化了，

许多年轻人爱上了古典妆容造型，他们都想体验一下，而且这股古风愈演愈烈。

王傲男说：“来成都之前我是有其他工作的，后来我把工作辞掉，专门来做与古代妆容有关的工作。我现在开了一家和汉服相关的淘宝店，日常也会出门给别的小姑娘画画古代的妆容。很感谢古代妆容让我发现新的自己，让我遇见更好的生活。都说‘女为悦己者容’，但是我觉得女孩子化妆应该是为了让自己发现更好的自己。女孩子小时候都会很向往古代的妆容，现在终于可以实现了。”

中国女性在各个时代的妆容千变万化，但她们的爱美之心不曾改变。东方之美不仅有含蓄内敛，也有如唐妆般的浓艳热烈。唐代女子大胆开放、自由独立的人生态度体现着中国文化的包容和进取。美不仅来自于化妆，更来自于内外兼修得来的

自信与智慧。红妆，妆点的不仅是女孩子们的面容，也表现出她们对于美好生活的向往与追求。今天，女性妆饰除了彰显自己的个性外，更多承载的是女性表达自我和对外界事物的看

法，她们最在意的不再是被男性关注，而是更看重在自我认同之下对美的表达。从传统的“女为悦己者容”到现代的“女为悦己而容”是社会进步的一种体现。

SCAN FOR A VIDEO

Chapter 6
第六章

# Women's Mysterious Script

# 女書之迷

万象中国
CHINA BOUQUET
第二册
Book 2

# Women's Mysterious Script

Women have used the Women's Four-Character Classics to teach girls how to be intelligent and behave well. Women's songs have reverberated across the mountains in Jiangyong County, Jiangzhou City, Hunan Province, brimming with various emotions for hundreds of years. Their lyrics are inscribed on folding fans, handkerchiefs, and waistbands with a special type of script. It is quite astonishing that this script is exclusive to women. What secrets hide in this script?

In Jiangyong's history, there was a practice where young girls would find friends of similar ages to bond as sisters, known as *laotong*. They exchanged messages in *Nüshu*, akin to how good friends today might exchange diaries. When they married, their friends would sing *Nüshu* ballads. In the film *Snow Flower and the Secret Fan*, the characters Lily and Snow Flower, portrayed by Chinese actress Li Bingbing and South Korean actress Gianna Jun, respectively, are a pair of sworn sisters, also called *laotong*, during the Qing Dynasty (1616-1911). Their intertwined destinies and mutual attachment can be seen as a representation of that historical period.

*Nüshu* was like a holy book for women, passed from mother to daughter and sister to sister. However, when a woman passed away, her writings would be burned, resulting in few documents being handed down through the generations. The earliest evidence of *Nüshu* is a bronze coin dating back to the period of the Taiping Movement (1851-1864), a peasant uprising in southern China. Inscribed on the back of this coin were the words "all the women in the world are sisters" in *Nüshu*, a script that represented the social ideal of progressive women at that time. Zhao Liming, a 76-year-old expert specializing in *Nüshu* and a professor in the Chinese Department at Tsinghua University, has devoted her lifetime to studying it. She deduced that the reason why the coin from that time was inscribed with *Nüshu* scripts was that some women who used *Nüshu* joined the force of the Taiping Movement as it passed through Hunan Province and proceeded to Nanjing.

Jiangyong is located on the border between Hunan and Guangxi, a small and remote town hidden in the mountains. Due to its harsh living conditions, in ancient times, the central government limited its involvement to setting up official agencies to manage affairs or exiling ministers. Since Jiangyong was far from the central government's location, this provided ideal conditions for the birth of *Nüshu*.

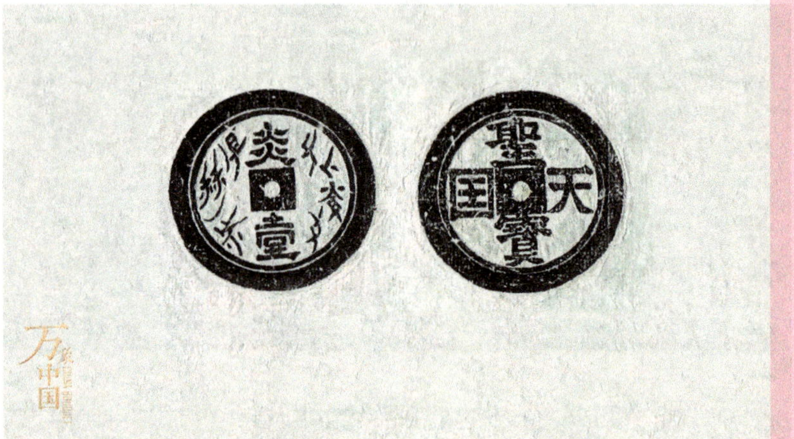

Jiangyong is where the Yao ethnic group is concentrated. This ethnic group in Jiangyong evolved from a matriarchal society. The Yao females are hardworking, audacious, and imbued with wisdom and creativity. Unlike the mainstream male-dominant culture in other places, females have a certain say and social status, which provides the cultural environment for the birth of *Nüshu*.

The geographical and cultural conditions facilitate the birth of *Nüshu*.

*Nüshu*, created by females, is solely used and passed down by them. In ancient times, women were not allowed to go to school. To depict their daily lives and express their inner feelings, the women in Hunan villages created this special script, *Nüshu*, drawing insights from Chinese characters, fully displaying their charm and wisdom.

The Chinese character, an ideographic writing system based on pictographs, is one of the oldest writing systems in the world. *Nüshu* evolved from Chinese characters. Unlike the ideographic writing of Chinese characters, *Nüshu* is a monosyllabic phonetic script pronounced in the Jiangyong local dialect, using about 500 characters to express the content fully.

The basic strokes of *Nüshu* are dots, vertical strokes, oblique strokes, and arcs. The pattern of *Nüshu* resembles that of the character 多, with the top right part higher than the lower left. The script is italicized,

resembling a rhombus. It is as tender as a soft willow swaying in the breeze, brimming with femininity. It is even nicknamed "long-feet script" or "mosquito-pattern script" by local women.

Most of *Nüshu* consists of poetic works that can be chanted. They are mostly seven-character verses, while only a few are five-character ones. The verses rhyme in every other line. They are often a mix of elegant and colloquial language, with exceptions in the character count and rhyme scheme.

*Nüshu* serves two main functions. First, it acts as a channel for females to express their inner emotions. Most *Nüshu* works feature women's inner feelings, such as the sufferings inflicted upon ancient women or their pent-up sadness and depression. Therefore, *Nüshu's* work is also called "bitter literature". In ancient times, men were allowed to venture out for business. At the same time, women could only find solace in their sworn sisters, sharing feelings, venting out emotions, and providing mutual relief via *Nüshu. Nüshu* offered females the chance to communicate with each other and share feelings and thoughts with their sisters to ease loneliness and find comfort in their minds.

Second, it serves as a means of expressing their daily lives. In ancient times, the women in Jiangyong were only allowed to do needlework and housework at home; therefore, they had more spare time. During their free time, they created *Nüshu*, which could be written on paper and folding fans to read for entertainment. This was a way of depicting their lives. During festivals or on their sisters' wedding days, they would gather to read *Nüshu*, sharing their lives and feelings.

Jiangyong women used their own script to tell stories, comfort each other, express sorrow, and give praise. They created a spiritual utopia for women.

In the 1950s, Zhou Shuoyi, a researcher in Jiangyong, discovered *Nüshu* while working in the local cultural center. This marked the beginning of the academia's focus on *Nüshu*. In 1982, Zhou included *Nüshu* in *The Chronicle of Cultural Relics in Jiangyong*, where it was named "long-feet mosquito-pattern character". Subsequently, Zhou collected a plethora of raw materials related to *Nüshu* locally. The *Collection of China's* Nüshu, compiled by Zhao Liming and annotated by Zhou Shuoyi, was published in 1992. Ji Xianlin, a well-known scholar in China, wrote a preface to the book, "When they were subjected to the suppression of theocracy, monarchy, clan and husband, leading lives akin to enslaved people, how could they learn? Almost all of them were illiterate and were deprived of the right to have their own names. However, they were not livestock but humans. They had thoughts and feelings, with a strong consciousness and the ability to distinguish right from wrong. They were eager to convey feelings and reveal their sorrows. But, since they knew nothing about characters, they had to create scripts with unique talent. They were like seedlings pressed beneath a big rock, yet they managed to find their way to see the light and the sun through tenacious efforts."

In 2004, Zhou Youguang, a well-known linguist in China, wrote a recommendation for *Nüshu* in its bid to be included in the World Intangible Cultural Heritage List: "*Nüshu* is like a wild rose hidden deep in the mountains of Chinese culture. It remained unknown to the public for a long time. Cultural explorers discovered the script only when it was on the brink of withering."

Tao Aimin, an artist whose work focuses on female themes, first learned about *Nüshu* in 2008. She felt she had discovered a new world and was eager to inject elements of this inspiration into her art. She traveled thousands of miles deep into the mountains to learn *Nüshu* from Hu Meiyue, one of the few inheritors. Hearing Hu's chanting, Tao said, "I think she experiences a kind of release to express herself freely when she speaks or sings in *Nüshu.* As all her feelings are conveyed through singing and narrating, she acquires a kind of freedom."

Afterward, she integrated *Nüshu* into her installation artworks. She collected several thousand washboards and created the artwork titled *Nüshu* by using the rubbing and traditional thread-binding method. She has a unique understanding of *Nüshu*, stating, "It has a special form, displaying softness and verve. Its pointed and oblique script style appears to point to the sky, emitting a unique scream. Each script seems to represent an individual spirit seeking freedom. It adds mystery to my work, *Nüshu*, making it reserved and profound. This work showcases a specific type of illegible visual language."

*Nüshu* is the only female-specific script in the world, known as the "miracle in the history of Chinese characters". This is because China has a diversified and inclusive writing system. *Nüshu* is the result of the fusion of Confucian culture and ethnic minority customs.

# 女书之谜

“四字女经，教尔聪明，娘边做女，莫出闺门。”数百年来，湖南省江州市江永县的大山中回荡着女性的歌声，歌声唱出了她们生命中的各种情感。这些歌谣用一种特殊的文字写在折扇上、手帕上、腰带上……令人震惊的是，这些文字只在女性中间流传。这到底是怎样一种文字呢？

在古时候的江永，女孩子们从小就会找一个年龄相仿的女性朋友结拜成姐妹，称为“老同”。她们通过女书进行秘密交流和互动。在她们出嫁的时候，好友们则会唱着女书歌谣相送。电影《雪花与秘扇》中李冰冰和全智贤扮演的百合与雪花正是清代一对结拜的“老同”，她们彼此命运的连结和相互的情感牵绊可以说是对那段历史的某种再现。

女书，如同属于女人的《圣经》，母传女，姐传妹，人死书焚，因此流传下来的文献资料很少。现存最早的女书物证是太平天国运动时期的一枚铜币，上面用女书刻着“天下妇女，姊妹一家”。76岁的女书研究专家、清华大学中文系教授赵丽明和女书打了大半辈子交道。她推测，太平天国运动的起义队伍途经湖南时，有使用女书的女性加入并一同抵达南京，才会在当时的铜币上留下女书字样。

江永地处湖南、广西两省交界处，是一座藏匿于崇山峻岭间的偏远小县。这里生存环境恶劣，古时历代中央政府除在这里设立官府办事和流放罪臣之外，几乎没有任何涉足。正因如此，江永县这样远离中央政权的偏僻之地才为女书的诞生提供了地理土壤。

江永是少数民族瑶族的聚居地。江永瑶族原本由母系氏族社会演化而来，瑶族女性有着瑶族人民特有的勤劳、勇敢、智慧和创造力。江永偏离主流的男权文化，女性具有一定的话语权和社会地位，这是女书诞生的文化环境。

在这种特殊的地理环境与文化环境下，诞生了女书这种独特的文字。

女书，由女性发明、女性使用、女性传承。古时候，女性不能进学堂。而潇水之滨、湖南乡村的女子为了表达自己的个人生活，宣泄内心的情感，大胆借鉴汉字，并运用她们的魅力和智慧创造了女书这种特殊的文字。

汉字是世界上最古老的文字之一，是以象形为基础的表意文字。女书由汉字演化而来，与汉字不同的是，女书是单音节的表音文字，记录的是江永当地方言，约500个字就可以完整

地表述她们想表达的内容。

女书的基本笔画是点、竖、斜、弧。女书字的外形呈“多”字式体势，右上高左下低，字形为斜体和菱形，清秀如弱柳扶风，有着女性的温柔气质，当地的妇女把它叫作“长脚文”或“蚊形字”。

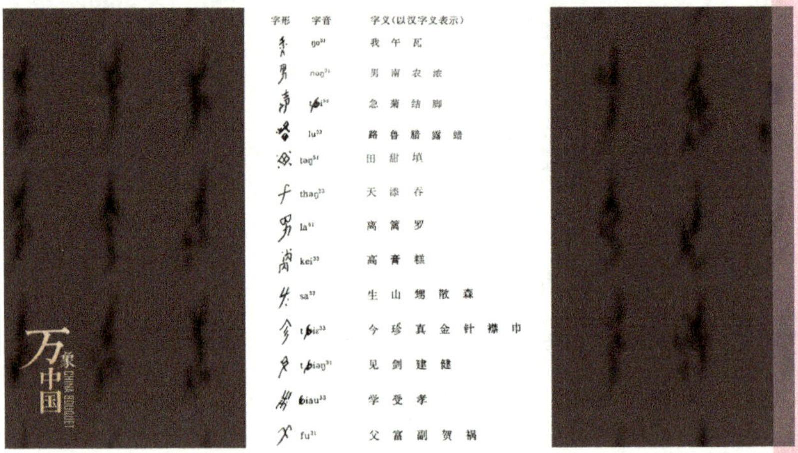


女书大都是能唱的诗体作品，女书作品多为七言韵文，少数为五言韵文，隔句押韵，用语雅俗夹杂，字数与韵脚也常有例外。

女书的作用主要有两种。首先，它是女性宣泄内心的情感的渠道。女书中最多的就是表达以女性内心情感为主的抒情题材，如讲述古代妇女的苦难遭遇和内心的悲苦压抑，因此女书文学又被称为“苦情文学”。在古代，男子可以出门闯天下，而女子只能结拜姐妹，通过女书交流情感，宣泄情绪，互相慰藉。正是女书，给了这些女性相互交流的机会，将心中所感所想与自己的姐妹分享，以此来安抚自己孤独的心灵，寻求精神的满足。其次，它是女性表达个人生活的手段。古时候，江永妇女只能在家做女红和家务。因此，她们有着更多可以自由支配的时间。在闲暇时，她们创造出了女书这种特殊的文字媒介，用来读纸读扇，互娱互乐，是表达个人日常生活的一种手段。在节日里，尤其是姐妹出嫁的日子里，大家聚在一起唱读女书，交流生活，倾诉情感。

江永女性用自己的文字倾诉并得到慰藉，唱出悲苦、相互赞美，构建了一个女性特有的精神王国。

20世纪50年代，江永本地研究者周硕沂在县文化馆工作时发现女书文字，这成为学界关注女书的起点。1982年，周硕沂将女书以“长脚蚊字”之名写进《江永文物志》中。后来，周硕沂在当地收集了许多女书原始材料。1992年，由他译注、赵丽明主编的《中国女书集成》出版。季羡林为该书写了序言:“她们在神权、君权、族权、夫权的四重压迫下，过着奴隶般的生活。哪里还谈得上什么学习呢？她们几乎统统是文盲，连起一个名字的权利都被剥夺，但是她们也是人，并不是牲畜。她们有思想，有感情，能知觉，善辨识。她们也想把这些感情表露出来，把自己的痛苦倾吐出来；但又苦于没有文字的工具，于是就运用自己独特的才识，自己创造文字。宛如一棵被压在大石头下的根苗，曲曲折折，艰苦努力，终于爬了出来，见到了天光，见到了太阳。”

2004年，周有光为女书申请世界遗产名录写下这样的推荐语：“女书，是中国文化深山里的一朵野玫瑰，它长期躲避了世俗眼光，直到它即将萎谢的最后时刻，才被文化探索者发现。”

2008年，一直以女性题材进行创作的艺术家陶艾民第一次知道了女书。她仿佛发现了新的天地，急切地想把这种灵感注入自己的艺术创作。于是，她不远千里来到大山深处，跟随女书传承人胡美月学习女书。在听了胡美月的吟唱后，她说："我在想，她在唱女书的时候能得到一种倾诉、一种释放，把自己的故事都唱出来、说出来。这就是一种通向自由的境界。"

后来，她将女书运用到她的装置艺术上。她收集了上千个搓衣板，用拓印和传统线装书结合的形式创作了一件题为《女书》的作品。对于女书，她有着一独一无二的理解，她说："它的特有形式，阴柔中暗藏着锐气，尖而斜的字体仿佛将矛头指向天空，发出另类的声音。它是一个个独立而向往自由的灵魂，它为我的《女书》增添了神秘气息，既含蓄而又深邃，呈现的完全是一种不可阅读的视觉语言。"

女书，是世界上唯一的女性专用文字，被誉为"中国文字史上的奇迹"。这得益于中国拥有多元包容的文字系统。女书是儒家文化和少数民族文化融合的产物。

SCAN FOR A VIDEO

Chapter 7
第七章

# Chasing in the Wind

万象中国

第二册

Book 2

# Chasing in the Wind

*Living in a Village*

*Grass grows, orioles soar, 'tis an early spring day,*
*The willows upon the dyke sway in balmy breezes.*
*The children return from school, not a moment behind,*
*They take to the fields, flying kites in the vernal wind.*

*—By Gao Ding*

*—Translated by Qin Dachuan*

The poem from the Qing Dynasty (1616-1911) depicts how a group of children fly kites joyfully in the field after school in spring. Warm breeze, green willows, and kites swaying in the sky are childhood memories for many Chinese people.

From time immemorial until now, people have never ceased pursuing the dream of flying in the sky. The earliest record of kites in China dates back to the *muyuan* (literally "wooden kite") invented by

Mo Di in the Eastern Zhou Dynasty (770-256 BC). Legend has it that Mo Di finally created a large wooden bird using wooden boards through three years of trial and error. Although it only flew in the sky for one day, the wooden bird kite was a significant attempt.

Despite Mo's failure, his spirit and crafting methods have been handed down. Later, Lu Ban, Mo Di's disciple, improved the kite by replacing the wooden board with bamboo. He even crafted a magpie-pattern kite, also called a "bamboo magpie", by polishing and roasting the bamboo to make it foldable. The refined kite could fly in the sky for three days this time.

Initially, kites were mainly used for military purposes. It is said that Han Xin, a general from the Han Dynasty (206 BC-AD 220), once used the kite for measuring. Emperor Wudi of Liang in the Southern and Northern Dynasties (420-589) sent messages through kites. During the Tang Dynasty (618-907), the kite was also used by General Zhang Pi to send a signal for help when he was besieged. From the Tang Dynasty onwards, the kite evolved into a toy. By the end of the Tang Dynasty, some kites were fixed with sound-producing devices made of strands or bamboo flutes. As the wind came, the kites would emit sound. Thus, they earned the Chinese name *fengzheng*, which means "wind-stringed musical instrument".

Wooden board, bamboo, and cowhide were the main materials used in kites until the Eastern Han Dynasty (25-220). After Cai Lun in the dynasty invented paper, their materials were gradually replaced with paper and silk. At that time, due to the high cost of *xuan*

paper, most kites were only made of bamboo paper with low elasticity. With the paper cost declining during the Ming and Qing dynasties, the real paper kite, also called *zhiyuan* in Chinese, began to gain popularity among the public.

In ancient times, the kites flown at different times indicate special cultural connotations. During the Qingming Festival, flying kites against wind was called *fangyu* (literally releasing repressed feelings) because it is not only a way of dispelling bad luck and relieving ailments but also a moment to remember the deceased. During harvest, flying kites also shows people's appreciation for the good weather and their pursuit of better lives.

Flying kites, as a recreational activity, is helpful for strengthening the body. A Chinese saying goes like this, "The whole year's work consists of a good start in spring." According to traditional Chinese medicine, spring is the best season to fly kites because flying kites in the open air in this warm and blossom season can effectively alleviate the internal heat accumulated in the body throughout the winter, help to stretch the bones and muscles, and improve health.

Over the past 2,000 years, numerous flying techniques and kite styles have emerged. The circling eagle kite is one of them.

Zhang Jinbiao is a track and field coach. Kites have become part of his life. He likes kites, but his are quite different from the others. They can fly even without a breeze and are called "circling eagle kites". Zhang Jinbiao said, "For this type of kite, you must pay attention to the framework. The horizontal and vertical lines must be strictly straight and symmetrical. It is really imitating the skeletal structure of an eagle." The circling eagle kite is evolved from traditional Chinese kites. It takes great skill to fly it and simulate an eagle circling above. The kite features a bamboo framework covered by paper. Accompanied by the music, Zhang flies the kite with his left hand rotating the wheel and right hand slightly pulling the string attached to the eagle kite. When it soars into the sky, it looks as if a real eagle is hovering in the sky.

Zhang Jinbiao used his knowledge of track and field to explore the relationship between kites and his movements, and this combination has brought him great joy. While flying a kite, he acted smoothly, and the eagle kite in his hands seemed real, which often attracted real eagles to play alongside it.

Nowadays, the adjustment made by the dexterous craftsmen makes the kites look lifelike, as if possessed of a spirit.

You can find bamboo across China. Indigenous people have used bamboo to make all sorts of daily tools and utensils. The framework of Chinese kites is also made of bamboo. It is a strong material, and bamboo is also remarkably flexible and can withstand strong winds without breaking. Craftsmen skillfully use fire to process bamboo. This simple method can produce complex shapes, which is quite ingenious.

Liu Baohua is a Chinese referee of kite-flying competition. One of his hobbies is making kites; thus, he prepares all the tools for making kites. His kite studio is in his own home. Although it is small and ordinary, the kites that are made in it are quite extraordinary.

Liu Baohua was born in Tianjin, a cradle of Chinese folk art. Kite-making is one of the most distinguished traditions of this region.

Liu Baohua said that he always wanted to make something different from traditional kites. He made a dynamic kite by installing levers and rotating wheels to make it alive.

Liu said, "By pulling levers and rotating gears, it creates a very dynamic effect. When it is up in the air, you can see that some parts come alive."

Although the principles are simple, making bamboo into precise mechanical parts is not easy. Liu Baohua uses his fine art skills to draw blueprints and then processes the parts according to the drawings. These dynamic kites with moving parts can be assembled through a series of strict processes.

Most of the kite's motion designs are inspired by ordinary things, and the kites are Liu's way of telling these everyday stories in the sky.

How mighty the crab kite he makes is as its eyes turn around in the breeze with its claws opening and closing alternately. His frog and tadpole kite is also impressive. Several adorable tadpoles follow their frog mother, wriggling in the breeze, while the frog mother pedals in the sky nonstop with her big eyes twinkling and seems to swim there heartily. He also makes a kite named "Laozi Went out of Hangu Pass", which is an allusion of Laozi, a famous philosopher in ancient China.

When the kite is flying, the Tai Chi graphic on Laozi's head keeps rotating with the legs of the ox he rides fluttering, creating the visual effect of running. His ingenuity makes kites come alive.

Kites have been flown for over two thousand years in China. They embody people's dreams about flying and demonstrate Chinese craftsmanship and ingenuity. Traditional Chinese kites are made of bamboo and paper in the shape of creatures and painted in colors to wish for happiness and auspiciousness. By flying kites swaying in the sky, the Chinese find a sense of freedom to roam between heaven and earth and among all creatures, which is a poetic expression of their optimistic, open-minded, and romantic spirit.

# 引线乘风

“草长莺飞二月天，拂堤杨柳醉春烟。儿童散学归来早，忙趁东风放纸鸢。”这是清代诗人写的一首诗，描绘的是春天里一群儿童放学后在田野里开心地放飞风筝的情景……暖暖的春风，嫩绿的杨柳，空中摇曳的风筝，这是多少中国人梦中难忘的童年。

从古至今，人们渴望在天空中翱翔的执念从未停止过。中国最早的关于风筝的记载可以追溯到春秋战国时期东周人墨翟制造的木鸢。传说墨翟潜心研究三年，通过不断地调试和研制，最终用木板制成了一只大木鸟，虽然大鸟只飞了一天，但也是对风筝研制的一次伟大尝试。

虽然墨翟没有成功，但是他的精神和研制的方法却流传了下来。后来，墨翟的学生鲁班改进了墨翟风筝的弊端，将风筝的材质由木板改为竹子，同时还把竹子削光滑，经过烤火折弯等方式，制作出一个喜鹊的形状，并称之为“木鹊”。这一次，经过改动后的风筝在高空翱翔了三天之久。

最开始，风筝主要用于军事。据说汉朝大将韩信曾利用风筝进行测量，梁武帝时曾利用风筝传信，唐朝的张丕被围困时曾利用风筝发出求救信号，等等。从唐朝开始，风筝逐渐变成玩具。到了晚唐，风筝上已有用丝条或竹笛作成的响器，风吹声鸣，因而有了“风筝”这个名字。

直到东汉之前，风筝的主要材料还只是木板、竹子以及牛皮。东汉蔡伦发明造纸术之后，风筝的材料逐渐变成纸和丝绢。由于当时宣纸的成本过高，大部分风筝的原材料依旧只能用韧性差的竹纸。直到明清时期纸张成本降低之后，真正的纸鸢才开始在百姓中盛行。

古时候每个时间段所放的风筝都被赋予了特殊的意义。清明时节的风筝，民间称之为“放郁”，迎风放出风筝，是对自身晦气病痛的放逐，更是对已故之人的思念。丰收时节的风筝，是对时年风调雨顺的感谢，更是对美好生活的祝愿和向往。

放风筝在娱乐身心的同时，更有利于强健人们的体魄。俗话说“一年之计在于春”。根据中医学的理论，春天是最适合放风筝的季节。在春暖花开之际去户外放风筝可以有效缓解冬季遗留在身体内的积热，更好地舒展筋骨，增强体质。

经过两千多年的发展，如今，风筝已经出现了许多新的玩法和样式。盘鹰风筝就是其中一种。

张金彪是一名田径教练，而风筝也是他生活的一部分。他喜欢风筝，但是他的风筝和别人不一样，没有风也可以飞起来，这种风筝就是盘鹰风筝。张金彪说：“盘鹰风筝的骨架设计讲究点点对称，横平竖直，它更多的是去模仿真鹰的骨架结构。”盘鹰是由中国传统风筝进化而来的，靠高超的技巧模拟鹰在天空中飞行。张金彪左手握轮，右手执鹰，音乐一起，只见他转动圆轮、轻拉细线，那鹰忽而一飞冲天，忽而掠地而过，这以竹为骨、以纸为肤的风筝仿佛有了生命一般。

张金彪用自己的田径知识去探索风筝与肢体运动的关系，沉迷在风筝给他带来的快乐中。他的动作如行云流水，他手中的盘鹰惟妙惟肖，真假难辨，还常常引来真鹰与它争斗玩耍。这时候的他手里拿的好像就是一只真鹰。

现在的能工巧匠们在风筝原来的形态上加了一些巧妙的心思，可以让风筝飞起来活灵活现，仿佛有了灵魂。

中国是竹子的王国，竹子的分布非常广泛，人们常常就地取材，用竹子制作各种生活用品。中国的风筝就是用竹子来做骨架的。竹子不仅有足够的强度，而且还有出色的韧性，可以承受强大的风力且不易折断。巧妙地利用火对竹子进行加工，

这种简单的方法可以令工匠们随心所欲地制作出造型复杂、巧妙的作品。

刘宝华是一位中国风筝裁判员，他的一大爱好就是做风筝。为此他给自己置办了全套的制作工具。刘宝华的风筝工作室就设在自己家中，虽然空间很小，但从这里制作出来的风筝却不一般……

刘宝华是天津人，天津是中国民间艺术的圣地，风筝是天津民间艺术中的绝活之一。

刘宝华说自己总想做一些与传统风筝有区别的东西。他制作的动态风筝通过拉杆、齿轮等巧妙的机关设计产生了活灵活现的效果。

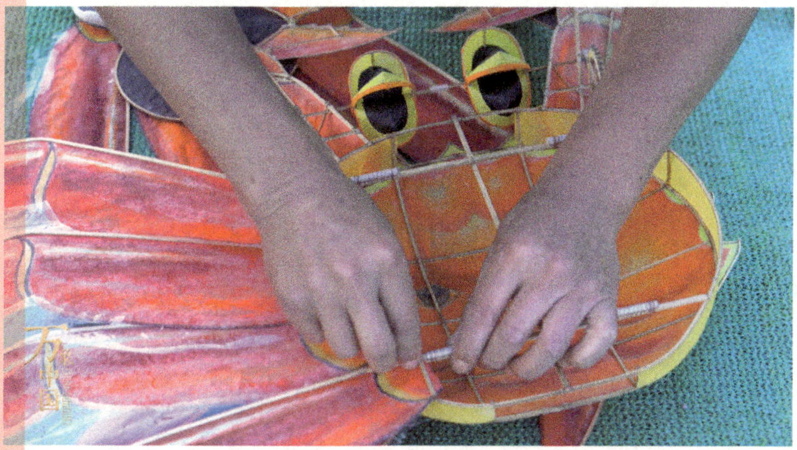

刘宝华说："通过拉杆，通过齿轮传动，可以产生一种特别灵动的效果，你会看到，飞到空中之后，它的某些部分是活灵活现的。"

原理虽然简单，但要想把竹子制作成精密的传动机件并不容易。刘宝华利用他的绘画天赋自己设计图纸，然后按照图纸进行加工。经过一道道严格的工序，千变万化的动态风筝就这样做出来了。

刘葆华设计的动态风筝大多来自生活中常见的事物，把这些故事搬上天空是刘宝华对风筝的独特解读。

他做的螃蟹风筝，螃蟹的眼睛在风中咕噜咕噜地转，钳子一张一合，好不威风；他做的小蝌蚪找妈妈风筝，几只可爱的小蝌蚪在风中一摇一摆地跟在青蛙妈妈后面，而青蛙妈妈的大眼睛一眨一眨的，四条腿不停地蹬着，好像在空中尽情地游

泳；他做的老子出关风筝，老子头上的太极在风中转个不停，青牛的腿在风中飘动，飞行时仿佛在奔跑。这些巧妙的心思，让风筝活了起来。

风筝在中国已经有超过2000年历史了，它寄托着中国人飞翔的梦想，体现着中国人精巧的匠心。中国人以一线摇曳于天际的风筝拟物赋彩，祈福纳祥，感受悠游于天地万物的心境，表达乐天旷达的浪漫情怀。

SCAN FOR A VIDEO

Chapter 8
第八章

# Three Generations of Shadow Puppeteers

# 皮影三代人

万象中国

CHINA BOUQUET

第二册

Book 2

# Three Generations of Shadow Puppeteers

*"—Monster, you dare ask who I am? I am Sun Long, the first disciple of the Stone God of Mount Tai. Monster, how dare you eat travelers on Mount Tai? I think you have lived long enough.*

*—Stop meddling and take my sword!"*

A puppet show entitled *Stone God and Canal Dragon Eliminate Evildoers to Protect Citizens* is being played in the Puppetry Theater of Tai'an in Shandong Province. A white curtain is used to divide the stage into two sections. The lights behind the curtain shine on it to display the images of thousands upon thousands of horses and soldiers and narrate numerous stories. Accompanied by traditional Chinese musical instruments and singing, the show exhibits a bustling scene. If you think there is a group working behind the curtain with several performers manipulating puppets, you will miss the point. Actually, there is only one person behind the curtain.

"While recalling the lyrics, the performer sings the tune with puppets waving in hand and feet stepping on the hammer." A performer must play several roles to complete a play by incessantly using five sensory organs, four limbs, and the brain. This is the superb, unique technique of Mount Tai Shadow Puppetry, called *shibuxian* (Do more than ten things at once).

There is a saying in the community of Chinese shadow puppetry, "While performing the puppetry, seven people are understaffed, nine are more than needed, and eight are the optimal choice." All puppetries in China are performed in groups except Mount Tai Shadow Puppetry, which a single person plays.

Mount Tai Shadow Puppetry is an ancient folk art, originating in Tai'an, Shandong Province, more than 600 years ago. What's unique about it is that one person performs the whole show. The performer holds the puppets in his hands, sings the dialogues, and controls eight musical instruments all by himself. This requires very fast movements and reactions and is known as the extraordinary technique of *shibuxian*.

Fan Zheng'an is a native of Tai'an. At the age of eight, he saw the puppet show for the first time. He was deeply impressed by the small figures who could fly into the sky and go beneath the earth on the white curtain while singing tunes to the accompaniment of boisterous music. At the sight of it, he fell in deep love. At the age of 13, he joined the folk art troupe in Tai'an, learning from puppeteer masters. He even became the sixth-generation inheritor of Mount Tai Shadow Puppetry. Since then, he has been fully engaged in the shadow puppet performance. Nowadays, at 78 years of age, he still has a booming voice and quick hands.

Mount Tai Shadow Puppetry features one person performing a whole play. In front of the stage, the audience can watch the lively scene where shadow figures fly up and down while listening to the funny accompaniment and tunes. However, there is only one performer behind the stage—Fan Zheng'an. He simultaneously manipulates eight musical instruments and different shadow figures by moving hands and feet. He performs while singing, coordinating all body parts to act like ten people performing together. Fan said, "The crux of *shibuxian* is multitasking in chorus by coordinating the movements of the mouth, feet, and hands. This performance is a testimony to one's skills and technique and a test of one's physical force. Each skill needs long-term practice."

Fan Zheng'an has a propensity for studying. Previously, the performer only had one traditional musical instrument called *muyu* close to his feet, hung drums and gongs on one side so that he had one hand to operate the puppets and the other to hit the drums and gongs. Later, he discovered a shortcoming in using this method of performing. If the puppets moved, there would be no drum and gong sounds, and vice versa. How could the puppets and musical instruments be operated at the same time? He thought of moving all the musical instruments to his feet. He designed where the musical instruments were placed before considering which tools were required to fix them and what techniques were needed to move feet. His past experiences of learning how to be a carpenter, being a fitter and painter came in handy. He drew sketches, tried different approaches, and practiced them by himself. Fan Zheng'an succeeded in the innovation in shadow puppetry based on the traditional performing skill of *shibuxian*. All the musical instruments were controlled by the feet while the puppets by hands. In this way, sound and image can be presented in a better way.

"We need to carry forward the handcraft left by our ancestors." Fan has kept making all the props and puppets by himself until now. In his eyes, modern machines cannot replace these traditional handcraft techniques. He is meticulous about choosing donkey hide, matching colors, sharpening gravers, and making wax tablets and wooden props.

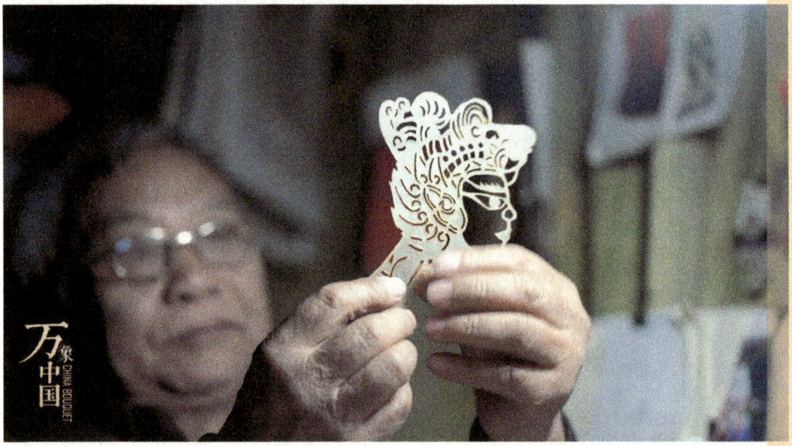

Nowadays, Fan Zheng'an is collecting and sorting out the materials in puppetry, hoping to hand down *shibuxian*. "Nowadays, I try to gather as many scripts, classical tunes, and puppetry methods as possible. And I want to make more puppets, all for a little museum, so the next generations can learn about *shibuxian* and pass it on."

Luckily, Fan Weiguo, the son of Fan Zheng'an, is the inheritor of the ancient art form. He graduated from the Central Academy of Fine Arts. Out of his deep passion for his family heritage, he has been exploring ways of developing Mount Tai Shadow Puppetry in the present day.

Fan Weiguo said, "What I do most now is to gradually integrate the art of Mount Tai Shadow Puppetry with our times. By combining it with people's lives today, so more young people can enjoy our art. This way, the art form can be better revitalized and passed on." Once, he contacted Tianleyuan, a centenary theater in Beijing, to discuss cooperation between shadow puppetry and the Peking Opera. In 2009, Fan Zheng'an recalled his son venturing out for business in Beijing back home. They self-funded and started a puppetry theater in Tai'an.

Fan Zheng'an has a fifteen-year-old grandson, Fan Fangyi, who is in middle school. At this age, he spends all his spare time learning to become a puppeteer. His grandfather is his best teacher.

Nowadays, Fan Fangyi has been nicknamed "Shadow Puppet Kid" since he has mastered this complex performance of *shibuxian*. Seeing his offspring follow in his footsteps, Fan Zheng'an was greatly inspired.

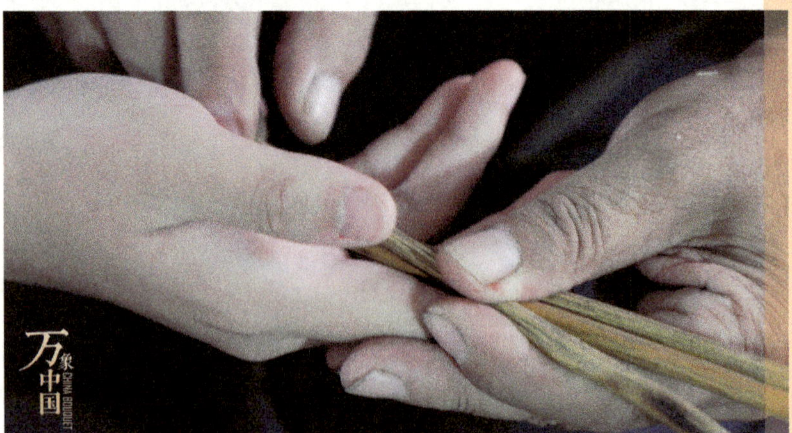

Fangyi's dream is to one day make an animated movie with shadow puppets. Under his family's influence and with a burning passion in his heart, Fan Fangyi, the eighth generation of Mount Tai Shadow Puppetry, is growing up.

Mount Tai Shadow Puppetry is a one-person show, but this craft requires the combined efforts of several generations. All the members of this big family are striving to pass on the art of Mount Tai Shadow Puppetry.

The Chinese people have a sense of duty toward their cultural heritage. Because of this love and persistence, the Chinese culture has lasted thousands of years.

# 皮影三代人

“妖怪，要问我？我是泰山石敢当的大徒弟孙龙。妖魔，你竟敢在泰山之上拦路吃人，我看你是活够了！

尔等竟然多管闲事，看刀——”

在山东泰安皮影研究院里正在上演皮影戏《石敢当运河龙为民除害保平安》。一张白色的幕布隔出台前台后两个空间，幕布后面有灯照来，幕布上映出千军万马，万千故事。整个戏吹拉弹唱，好不热闹。如果你以为幕布后有一个乐队在演奏，还有几个演员在操纵皮影，那可就错了——其实幕后面只有一个人！

“脑里想着词儿、嘴里唱着曲儿、手里舞着人儿、脚下踩着锤儿”，表演者五官、四肢、头脑一刻都不能闲着，一人身兼数职完成一整台戏的演出，这就是中国皮影最高超的古老绝

活——泰山皮影戏“十不闲”。

中国皮影界有“七紧、八松、九消停”的说法，意思是皮影戏表演八个人配合正好，七个人紧张，九个人就有人闲，基本上都是团队演出，只有泰山皮影戏是全国唯一的单人皮影戏。

泰山皮影600多年前兴起于山东泰安，是一种古老的民间艺术，它最大的特点是整个表演由一人独自完成。表演者双手拿着影人，嘴里唱着词，还要操纵八种乐器——这需要极快的反应与动作，被称为绝活“十不闲”。

范正安是地道的泰安人。8岁那年，他第一次看皮影。当他看到一块白白的布上小影人儿又能上天又能入地，还配着锣鼓喧天的音乐唱着曲儿……他被深深地吸引了。范正安对泰山皮影“一见钟情”，他13岁时加入泰安曲艺团，拜师学艺，成为泰山皮影第六代传承人，从此，一干就是一辈子。如今，他已经78岁高龄了，但仍然嗓音洪亮，手脚敏捷。

泰山皮影讲究的是“一个人一台戏”。台前，观众看着上下翻飞的影人，听着有趣的伴奏和唱腔，热闹非凡；而台后，

却是范正安一个人的舞台。他手脚并用同时操纵八样乐器和各种影人，自己边唱边演，协调地调动全身，一个人当十个人用。范正安说，“十不闲”最难的是一心多用，手脚口灵活配合，不仅是技巧和功力的体现，更是体力的考验，每项基本功都需要磨炼。

范正安好钻研。前人的“十不闲”脚上只有木鱼这一种乐器，而锣鼓是挂在一边，操作皮影时腾出一只手来击打。他发现这种方式有一个弱点：皮影动，就没有锣鼓声，有锣鼓声，皮影就不能动。怎么才能让皮影和乐器同时被操作呢？范正安想到了把乐器全部移到脚上。他先设计各种乐器摆放的位置，然后考虑固定乐器需要哪些工具，再琢磨脚上的操作技法。他早年学过的木匠、钳工、画图的手艺都派上了用场，先画出图来，然后自己动手做，一边想一边做一边练。终于，范正安在传统“十不闲”的基础上成功对皮影戏进行了革新：乐器都用脚来操控，手里只操作皮影，声音和形象兼顾。

“老祖宗传下来的手艺必须坚持。”到现在，范正安依然坚

持亲手制作所有的道具和影人。在他看来，这些传统的手工技艺是现代的机器生产不能代替的。选择驴皮、搭配色彩、打磨刻刀、制作蜡板，甚至影幕道具的木工活儿，他都做得一丝不苟。

现在，范正安正在做一些收集、整理的工作，希望把“十不闲”传下去。“我现在尽最大可能多整理一些剧本、唱腔、操作技能，多做一些皮影，办一个小型的博物馆，让我们的下一代年轻人更加直观、全面地了解这项优秀的传统艺术——‘十不闲’，把它发扬传承下去。”

幸运的是，这门古老的艺术后继有人，他就是范维国，范正安之子。毕业于中央美院的这个年轻人出于对家传技艺的热爱，不断探索着泰山皮影在当下的各种发展可能。

范维国说：“我现在做得最多的事就是把泰山皮影这门艺术逐渐和时代结合，和现在的生活结合，让更多的年轻人能够喜欢我们这门艺术，这样这门艺术才能更好地焕发活力，更好地生存和传承下去。”他曾经找过北京的百年戏院——天乐园，探讨皮影与京剧的跨界合作。2009年，范正安召回在北京闯荡的儿子，自筹资金在泰安市老县衙内创办了“泰山皮影研究院”小剧场。

范正安的孙子、15岁的范方一是一名中学生。在喜欢新鲜事物的年纪，他把学习之外的时间都用在了泰山皮影上。爷爷就是他最好的老师。

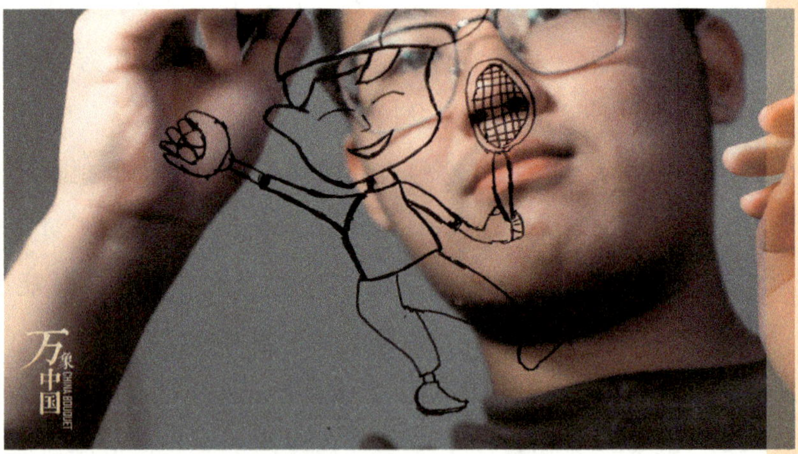

如今，被称为“皮影小子”的他已经可以独立完成“十不

闲”的表演。看着自己的手艺后继有人，范正安很是开心。范方一的梦想是未来用皮影做一部动画片。家庭的熏陶，内心的热爱，泰山皮影的第八代传人正在长大。

泰山皮影，是一个人的舞台，但这份事业却需要几代人共同的努力。这个大家庭的所有成员都在为泰山皮影的传承发展而付出。

中国人对自己的民族文化有一种发自内心的使命感。正是因为这份热爱与坚守，中国文化才得以在数千年里绵延流传，生生不息。

SCAN FOR A VIDEO

Chapter 9
第九章

# Redefinition of Kung Fu

# 功夫之道

万象中国
CHINA BOUQUET
第二册
Book 2

# Redefinition of Kung Fu

Speaking of kung fu, what comes to your mind first? Bruce Lee? Kung Fu Panda? Or Shaolin Temple?

Zhenguodong Temple, located in Quanzhou City of Fujian Province, is also called the Southern Shaolin compared to Shaolin Temple in Henan Province. Legend has it that Zhenguodong Temple was built by Zhikong, one of the 13 monks who had rescued the Tang Emperor. The temple is regarded as the birthplace of southern martial arts in China. There is an expression "southern style boxing and northern style leg" in Chinese martial arts, in which "southern style boxing" often refers to Taizu Boxing. It is said that this boxing style originated from Southern Shaolin, and it was not until the Ming Dynasty (1368-1644) that it developed into an independent boxing system.

泉州少林寺
Quanzhou Shaolin Temple

The Southern and Northern Shaolin share the same origin and are closely associated with each other. "See your nature, and you will become a Buddha." They advocate practicing meditation and martial arts, the integration of which attracts many followers here to learn martial arts.

On a summer evening in south China, it was sultry and humid with cicadas singing around. All the kids went to rest except for a boy named Zhizhen, who was practicing boxing. He moved quickly in a yellow costume with determined eyes, appearing vigorous. "Zhizhen, why are you still practicing?"asked his master with deep concern while seeing him still practicing. Zhizhen replied, "Because I want to be as good as you are." His diligence made the master full of joy. He began to guide the boy step by step, saying, "Kung fu is like eating a meal. You cannot just eat one mouthful and be full. Kung fu takes time, and time makes kung fu. Keep practicing day after day, and you will eventually get the answer you are looking for." The master and the disciple stood together, silhouetted against the sunset glow.

The highlight of Shaolin martial arts is the integration of meditation and martial arts, which means meditation starts before practicing martial arts. In contrast, martial arts facilitate the practice of meditation. The monks in Shaolin Temple practice martial arts in their daily routines, such as carrying water and sweeping floors. They improve daily and unknowingly become masters with superb skills one day.

A Chinese proverb goes, "A boxer must keep practicing boxing, and a singer singing." Practicing daily will help you be well-versed in a certain skill, a universal principle that can be applied to anything you do. Chinese calligrapher Wang Xizhi once practiced writing beside a pool all day, and no one would know how much ink he used and how many brushes were ruined. Since he had to clean the brushes in the pool, the water gradually turned into black ink after a long period. This is the "ink pool" people can see today in Shaoxing, Zhejiang Province.

Qi Baishi, a painting master, had been fond of seal cutting since young. One day, he visited a senior seal engraver and asked him to give some guidance on seal cutting. The engraver told him jokingly, "Please carry a bucket of stones back home and carve on all these stones before erasing them. Keep practicing till the stones turned into ashes. Only then can you master the seal cutting skills." Qi Baishi really did as the senior engraver told him. While cutting the seals, he compared his carvings with ancient ones to further hone his skills. As the days went on, stones grew less while ashes piled up on ground. It was not until the entire bucket of stones turned into ashes that Qi Baishi became a famous seal engraver.

In the Mogao Grottoes in Dunhuang, ancient painters worked day and night in dim caves, creating numerous works that Chang Shana, a contemporary painting artist, copies in caves repeatedly thousands of years later. *Xuan* paper-making masters produced paper piece by piece year after year to make top-notch paper through their skilled assessment of touch and texture. Huang's family was committed to weaving steamers from generation to generation, and thus, they were passed on and enjoyed a good reputation at home and abroad. Since the restorers took great pains to renovate the cultural relics in Palace Museum so that they can be seen again today. Due to his countless practices, the senior Fan Zheng'an acquired the extremely hard skill of shadow puppetry. The unique skill each of them possesses, which is their "kung fu", is the outcome of their

unyielding efforts. It is because of their tenacity and perseverance that the ancient Chinese skills and wisdom can be handed down till now.

As time elapsed, the ingenuity still exists. Until now, numerous Chinese people stick to their posts, doing the same job year after year to display their craftsmanship. They devote their lifetime to refining a certain job skill to breath life into it.

Chang Baozhong has been a chef for over 30 years, starting at the age of 18. Although he is now the head chef, he still arrives in the kitchen an hour early every morning to practice cutting skills and prepare for the day. Practice makes perfect. As with kung fu, he has to do it every day to keep his great skill.

Chang Baozhong says, "When cooking Chinese food, knife cutting skill is more important than time of firing. Chopping determines the visual presentation of a dish, as well as its texture and taste. This seemingly simple action requires a long period of practice; otherwise, you will get rusty."

Chinese cucumber salad is the dish every cook must master before becoming a chef because it reflects the skills of cutting. Each cut requires consistent pressure in order to achieve this very special effect. Chef Chang can extend a 30-centimeter-long cucumber to over 120 centimeters by cutting. His knife's rise and fall reflects over 30 years of kung fu (dedicated practice).

Zhao Pengcheng is a pharmacist at Kong Yi Tang Pharmacy, a TCM studio in Beijing, with a focus on filling prescriptions. Generally, a prescription contains more than a dozen herbs, and each herb dose has to be precisely weighed with an error margin of less than one gram. Zhao can complete the process of grabbing and packaging the prescription and handing it to the patients in just one minute. This kind of kung fu needs five to six years of unremitting practice.

The day's work is over. When one colleague said to him,"Bye! I'm off work," Zhao only gave a short reply and went on to practice his hand. Back at home, he still kept practicing. There were three kinds of herbs on his desk, namely, wolfberry, lily, and cinnamon, each with a different texture, weight, and feel. He held and weighed the herbs repeatedly using a small electronic scale to improve the accuracy.

Zhao Pengcheng said, “I know I’m young and lack experience in this area, so I have to work harder. My master taught me that there are no shortcuts on this road. If I want to do well, I must put in more time and energy than others. ”

Here, the pharmacist’s hand is the scale. Picking up the accurate amount not only guarantees work efficiency, but also relieves the patient of worry. Here, kung fu transforms an ordinary act into a superb skill.

In fact, kung fu is not a mystery. It is ordinary and it's all around us. Chinese have always paid attention to self-improvement and accumulation. Just like the "10,000-hour rule", Chinese people's kung fu is the result of their ceaseless efforts. It exists in all walks of life, and in this constant stream of people, you never know who might be the next Bruce Lee.

# 功夫之道

说起“功夫”，你会首先想到什么？Bruce Lee，功夫熊猫，还是少林寺？

福建泉州的镇国东禅寺，也称南少林——相对于河南的少林寺而言，相传为曾救唐王的十三棍僧之一的智空入闽所建。这里是中国南方武术的发源地。武术界有“南拳北腿”的说法，南拳指的是太祖拳，据说最初就是出于南少林，在明代才逐渐形成独立拳系。

南北少林，同宗同源，一脉相承。“直指人心观本性，见性成佛定禅宗”。崇禅尚武，在练武中修行，在修行中练武，这种精神吸引了很多人来这里学武。

南方夏天的傍晚潮湿闷热，蝉鸣声声，别的孩子都去休息了，只有一个叫志振的男孩儿还在练拳。他穿着一身黄色的练功服，闪展腾挪，目光坚定，颇有气势。“志振，你怎么到

现在还在练功啊？”他的师父理刚看到他在别人休息时还在练功，关心地问道。志振回答道：“因为我想练得像您一样厉害！”师父见他如此勤奋好学，心中甚是欢喜，就手把手地指导他。师父一边指导一边说：“功夫就像吃饭一样，一口吃不成个胖子。功夫就是时间，时间成就了功夫，日复一日，你终会得到你想要的答案。”师徒二人的身影在晚霞的余晖中映成一道剪影。

少林武术最突出的特点就是禅武合一，即以禅入武，习武修禅，因此又有“武术禅”之称。少林僧人就是在日常的行住坐卧中练功的，挑水是练功，扫地是练功，功夫在日复一日中进步，不知不觉就练成了绝世武功。

俗话说：“曲不离口，拳不离手。”只有每天练习，勤学苦练，才能使功夫日渐纯熟。无论做任何事都是这个道理。中国大书法家王羲之每天在池子边练字，送走黄昏，迎来黎明，不知写完了多少墨水，写烂了多少毛笔。他每天练完字就在池水里洗笔，天长日久竟将一池水都洗成了墨色，这就是人们今天在绍兴可以看到的传说中的“墨池”。

齐白石年轻时是个篆刻爱好者。一天，他向一位老篆刻家求教。老篆刻家开玩笑地说：“你去挑一担石头回家，刻了磨，磨了刻，等到这一担石头都变成了泥浆，那时你的印就刻好了。”齐白石真的去挑了一担石头回来，夜以继日地刻，一边刻一边拿古代篆刻艺术品来对照琢磨，刻了磨平，磨平了再刻。日复一日，年复一年，石头越来越少，而地上淤积的泥浆却越来越厚。最后，一担石头统统都化为泥浆，齐白石真的练成了大艺术家。

敦煌莫高窟的画工在昏暗的石窟里日复一日地画，千年后，常沙娜在石窟里一遍又一遍地临摹；制造宣纸的捞纸师父年复一年一张一张地捞，才能靠手感捞出品质上佳的宣纸；黄家一代又一代人都在编织蒸笼，黄家蒸笼才能世代相传，长销海内外；故宫里的文物修复师一点一点地修缮，才能使这些古老的器物得以重见天日；“十不闲”老人范正安无数次练习，才能练成这种高难度的皮影绝活……他们每个人都身怀绝技，

这就是他们的"功夫"，而正是坚持不懈的努力成就了他们这一身功夫。中国古老的智慧和技艺，就是靠这些人的顽强坚守才流传到今天，让我们与祖先血脉相连。

时光流转，匠心永驻。时至今日，无数个中国人依然在自己的岗位上慢慢地、静静地、经年累月地做同样的事，整个人和这件事精神互融。他们将一门技艺融入生命，也为这门技艺注入生命。

常保中，18岁开始学习烹饪，至今从业30余年。尽管已经身为厨师长，但他每天清晨仍然会提前一个小时到后厨练习刀功，准备配菜。像练功夫一样，只有每天坚持练习，他才能保持手法不生疏，记忆不丢失。

常保中说："做中餐，刀工比火候更重要。它不仅决定了一盘菜的视觉呈现，也关乎菜品的味道。而这看似简单的动作，却需要日积月累，经常练习，否则就会生疏。"

每个厨师在入行之前都需要通过"蓑衣黄瓜"这道菜的考核，因为它要求下刀深度一致才能长而不断，最能体现厨师的刀功。常大厨能把长30厘米的黄瓜连续不断切至120厘米。刀起刀落，都是这30余年功夫的写照。

赵鹏成是北京中医馆——孔医堂的药剂师，平时的工作就是给病人抓药。一张中药药方一般包含10余种药材，每种都要精确到1克，赵鹏成能在短短1分钟之内完成所有流程，把药抓配好并包装后交给患者。这样的功夫是连续五六年的不懈努力磨炼出来的。

下班时间到了，同事跟他说："下班了，我先走了啊！"赵鹏成应了一声，继续练习抓药。回到家后，赵鹏成仍然没有

停歇。他的案头放着三样药材——枸杞、百合、肉桂，它们的质地不同，重量与手感各异，他用一个小小的电子秤一遍一遍地捉取、称量，练习手感。

赵鹏成说："我知道自己很年轻，所以更要下功夫。师傅告诉我这条路上没有捷径，想要做好就得付出比别人更多的时间和精力。"

药剂师的手就如同一杆秤，精准地抓取不仅能保证工作效率，也能解除患者的担忧。功夫就这样从平凡中蜕变成一种精湛的技艺。

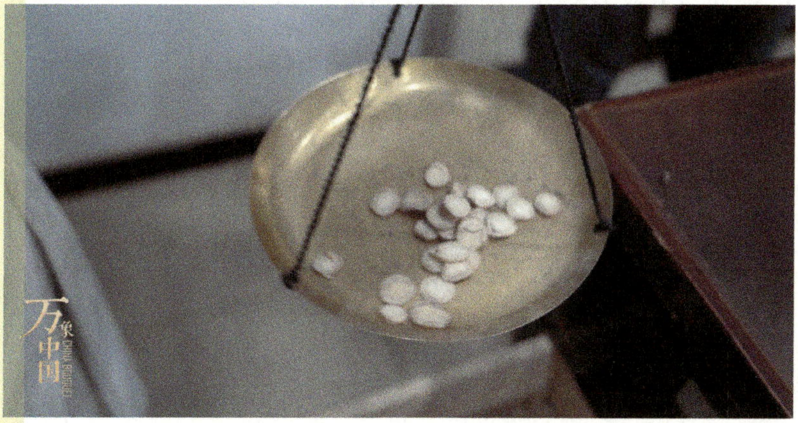

其实，功夫并不神奇，它就在我们身边。中国人素来讲究自强不息，厚积薄发。就如同"一万小时定律"，中国人的功夫存在于各行各业，是时间与坚持不懈的努力。在这川流不息的人群中，谁都有可能成为你这个行业的Bruce Lee。

SCAN FOR A VIDEO

出 品 人：王君校
策划编辑：张　超
责任编辑：陆　瑜
英文翻译：吴爱俊
英文编辑：吴爱俊
封面设计：张　颖
印刷监制：汪　洋

图书在版编目（CIP）数据

万象中国. 第二册：汉英对照 / 许柏成主编；杨晗编著. -- 北京：华语教学出版社, 2024.7
ISBN 978-7-5138-2513-9

Ⅰ. ①万… Ⅱ. ①许… ②杨… Ⅲ. ①汉语 - 对外汉语教学 - 语言读物 Ⅳ. ①H195.5

中国国家版本馆CIP数据核字（2024）第000379号

万象中国　第二册
许柏成 主编
杨　晗 编著
*

华语教学出版社有限责任公司出版
（中国北京百万庄大街24号　邮政编码　100037）
电话:（86）10-68320585　68997826
传真:（86）10-68997826　68326333
网址:　www.sinolingua.com.cn
电子信箱:　hyjx@sinolingua.com.cn
北京虎彩文化传播有限公司印刷
2024年（32开）第1版
2025年第1版第2次印刷
（汉英）
ISBN　978-7-5138-2513-9
008900